NATIONAL QUALIFIC
MODEL PAPER

Higher MATHEMATICS

ISBN 0 7169 9347 3

The model papers contained herein do not emanate from the Scottish Qualifications Authority. They are based on existing examination papers which have been modified to illustrate the proposed format of the Higher Still Higher Mathematics papers.

ROBERT GIBSON · Publisher
17 Fitzroy Place, Glasgow, G3 7SF.

CONTENTS

INSTRUCTIONS TO CANDIDATES 3

FORMULAE LIST 4

MODEL PAPER A Paper I 5
Paper II 9

MODEL PAPER B Paper I 14
Paper II 18

MODEL PAPER C Paper I 24
Paper II 28

MODEL PAPER D Paper I 35
Paper II 39

MODEL PAPER E Paper I 46
Paper II 51

MODEL PAPER F Paper I 56
Paper II 61

MODEL PAPER G Paper I 67
Paper II 72

ANSWERS 77

FREQUENCY CHART 88

NATIONAL
QUALIFICATIONS

MATHEMATICS
HIGHER

INSTRUCTIONS TO CANDIDATES

PAPER 1 — 1 hour 10 minutes

(Non-calculator)

1. **Calculators may NOT be used in this paper.**
2. Full credit will be given only where the solution contains appropriate working.
3. Answers obtained by readings from scale drawings will not receive any credit.

PAPER 2 — 1 hour 30 minutes

1. **Calculators may be used in this paper.**
2. Full credit will be given only where the solution contains appropriate working.
3. Answers obtained by readings from scale drawings will not receive any credit.

FORMULAE LIST

Circle:

The equation $x^2 + y^2 + 2gx + 2fy + c = 0$ represents a circle centre $(-g, -f)$ and radius $\sqrt{g^2 + f^2 - c}$.

The equation $(x - a)^2 + (y - b)^2 = r^2$ represents a circle centre (a, b) and radius r.

Scalar Product: $\boldsymbol{a}.\boldsymbol{b} = |\boldsymbol{a}|\,|\boldsymbol{b}| \cos \theta$, where θ is the angle between $\boldsymbol{a}$ and $\boldsymbol{b}$

or $\boldsymbol{a}.\boldsymbol{b} = a_1b_1 + a_2b_2 + a_3b_3$ where $\boldsymbol{a} = \begin{pmatrix} a_1 \\ a_2 \\ a_3 \end{pmatrix}$ and $\boldsymbol{b} = \begin{pmatrix} b_1 \\ b_2 \\ b_3 \end{pmatrix}$.

Trigonometric formulae:

$$\sin (A \pm B) = \sin A \cos B \pm \cos A \sin B$$

$$\cos (A \pm B) = \cos A \cos B \mp \sin A \sin B$$

$$\sin 2A = 2\sin A \cos A$$

$$\cos 2A = \cos^2 A - \sin^2 A = 2\cos^2 A - 1 = 1 - 2\sin^2 A$$

Table of standard derivatives and integrals:

$f(x)$	$f'(x)$
$\sin ax$	$a\cos ax$
$\cos ax$	$-a\sin ax$

$f(x)$	$\int f(x)\,dx$
$\sin ax$	$-\frac{1}{a}\cos ax + C$
$\cos ax$	$\frac{1}{a}\sin ax + C$

NATIONAL QUALIFICATIONS

MODEL PAPER A

MATHEMATICS HIGHER

Paper 1
(Non-calculator)

Refer to page 3 for Instructions to Candidates

All questions should be attempted

Marks

1. A is the point (–3, 2, 4) and B is (–1, 3, 2). Find

(a) the components of vector $\overrightarrow{AB}$; **(1)**

(b) the length of AB. **(2)**

2. Relative to the axes shown and with an appropriate scale, Alex stands at the point (–2, 3) where Hartington Road meets Newport Road.

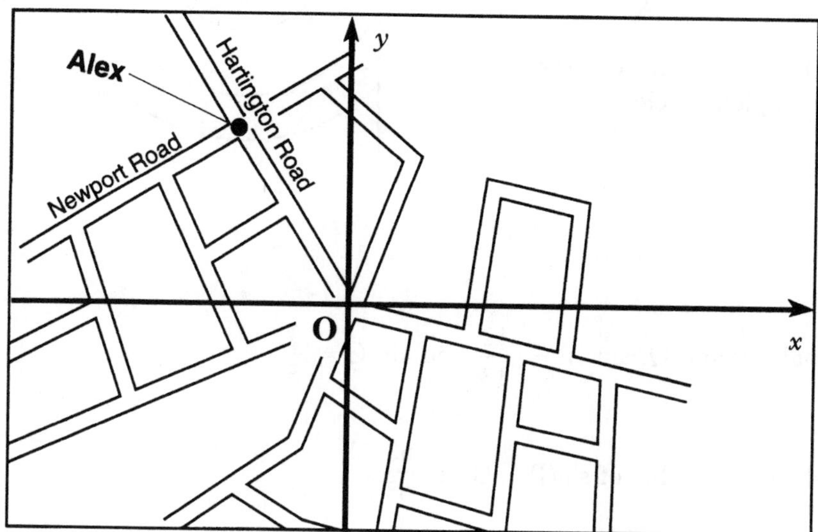

(a) Find the equation of Newport Road which is perpendicular to Hartington Road. **(3)**

(b) Brenda is waiting for a bus at the point (–5, 1). Show that Brenda is standing on Newport Road. **(2)**

Marks

3. The graphs of $y = f(x)$ and $y = g(x)$ intersect at the point A on the y-axis, as shown on the diagram.

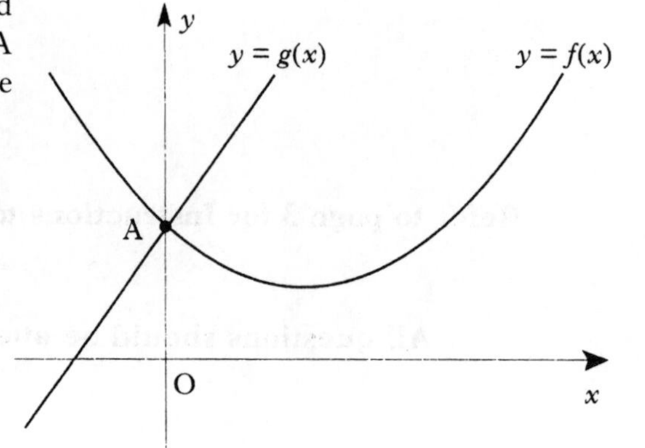

If $g(x) = 3x + 4$ and $f'(x) = 2x - 3$, find $f(x)$. **(4)**

4. In an experiment with a ripple tank, a series of concentric circles with centre C(4, −1) is formed as shown in the diagram.

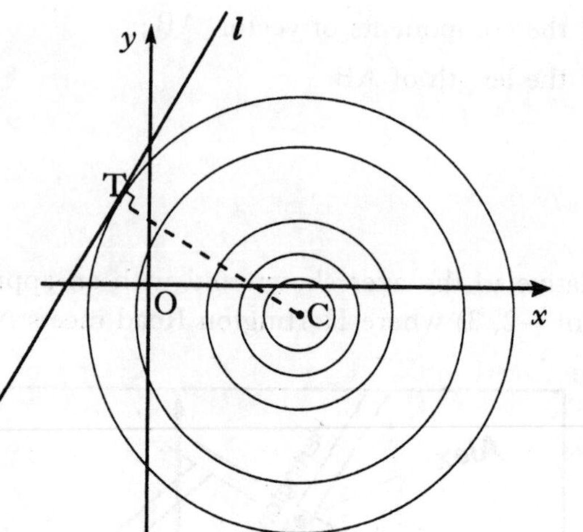

The line $\boldsymbol{l}$ with equation $y = 2x + 6$ represents a barrier placed in the tank.

The largest complete circle touches the barrier at the point T.

(a) Find the equation of the radius CT. **(3)**

(b) Find the equation of the largest complete circle. **(5)**

5. For acute angles P and Q, $\sin P = \dfrac{12}{13}$ and $\sin Q = \dfrac{3}{5}$.

Show that the **exact** value of $\sin(P + Q)$ is $\dfrac{63}{65}$. **(4)**

Marks

6. One root of the equation $2x^3 - 3x^2 + px + 30 = 0$ is -3.

Find the value of p and the other roots. **(4)**

7. The diagram shows the graph of $y = f(x)$.

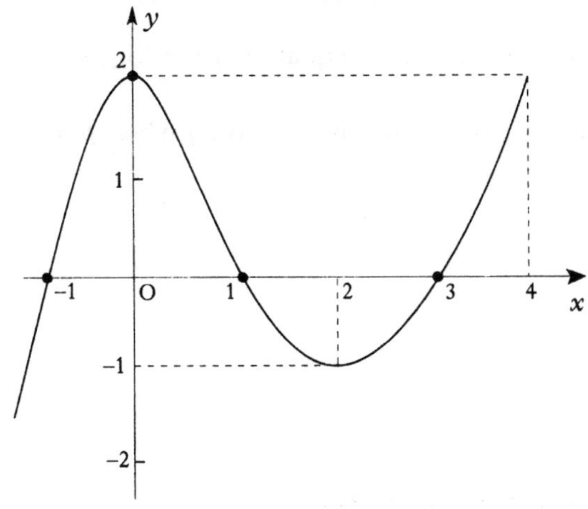

Sketch the graph of $y = 2 - f(x)$. **(3)**

8. Differentiate $4\sqrt{x} + 3\cos 2x$. **(4)**

9. *(a)* Show that $(\cos x + \sin x)^2 = 1 + \sin 2x$. **(2)**

(b) Hence find $\int (\cos x + \sin x)^2 dx$. **(4)**

Marks

10. Find $\int \sqrt{1+3x}\,dx$ and hence find the **exact** value of $\int_0^1 \sqrt{1+3x}\,dx$. **(5)**

11. The point P(p, k) lies on the curve with equation $y = \log_e x$.

The point Q(q, k) lies on the curve with equation $y = \frac{1}{2}\log_e x$.

Find a relationship between p and q and hence find q when $p = 5$. **(4)**

[END OF QUESTION PAPER]

Refer to page 3 for Instructions to Candidates

All questions should be attempted

Marks

1. The function f, whose incomplete graph is shown in the diagram, is defined by $f(x) = x^4 - 2x^3 + 2x - 1$. Find the coordinates of the stationary points and justify their nature. **(7)**

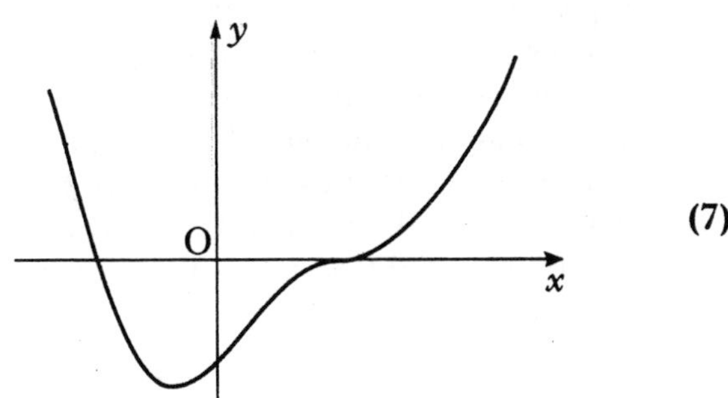

2. The concrete on the 20 feet by 28 feet rectangular facing of the entrance to an underground cavern is to be repainted.

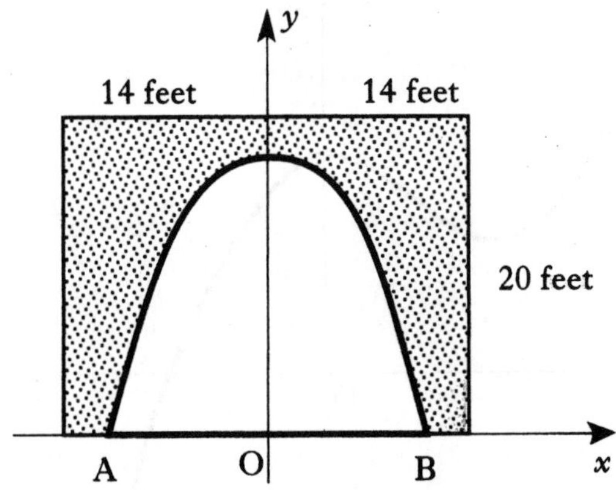

Coordinate axes are chosen as shown in the diagram with a scale of 1 unit equal to 1 foot. The roof is in the form of a parabola with equation $y = 18 - \frac{1}{8}x^2$.

(a) Find the coordinates of the points A and B. **(2)**

(b) Calculate the total cost of repainting the facing at £3 per square foot. **(4)**

Marks

3. $f(x) = 2x - 1$, $g(x) = 3 - 2x$ and $h(x) = \frac{1}{4}(5 - x)$.

(*a*) Find a formula for $k(x)$ where $k(x) = f\big(g(x)\big)$. **(2)**

(*b*) Find a formula for $h\big(k(x)\big)$. **(2)**

(*c*) What is the connection between the functions h and k? **(1)**

4. The diagram shows the plans for a proposed new racing circuit. The designer wishes to introduce a slip road at B for cars wishing to exit from the circuit to go into the pits. The designer needs to ensure that the two sections of road touch at B in order that drivers may drive straight on when they leave the circuit.

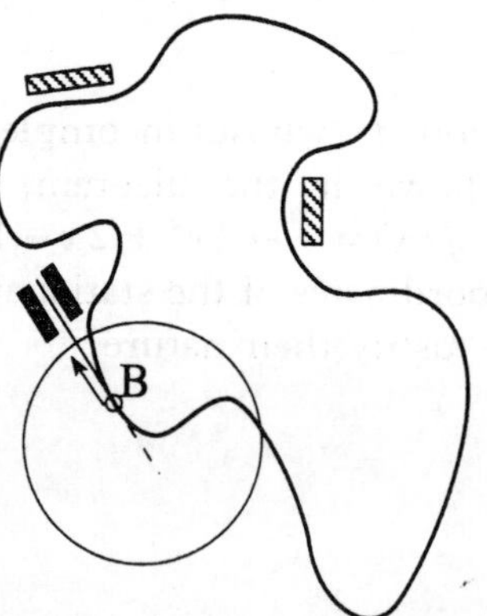

Relative to appropriate axes, the part of the circuit circled above is shown below. This part of the circuit is represented by a curve with equation $y = 5 - 2x^2 - x^3$ and the proposed slip road is represented by a straight line with equation $y = -4x - 3$.

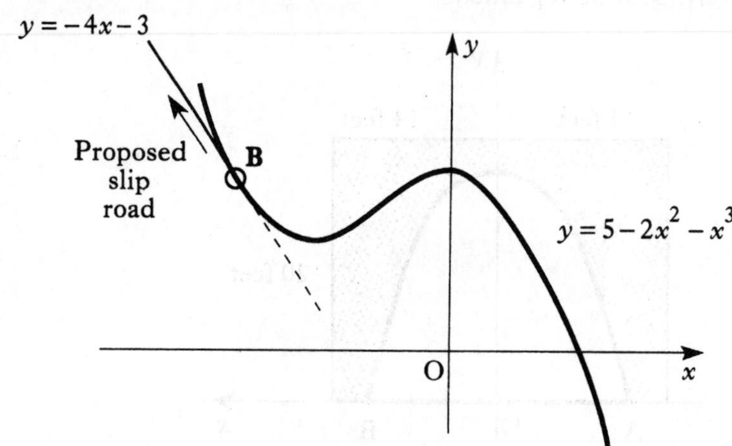

(*a*) Find algebraically the coordinates of B. **(4)**

(*b*) Justify the designer's decision that this direction for the slip road does allow drivers to go straight on. **(1)**

Marks

5. Secret Agent 004 has been captured and his captors are giving him a 25 milligram dose of a truth serum every 4 hours. 15% of the truth serum present in his body is lost every hour.

(a) Calculate how many milligrams of serum remain in his body after 4 hours (that is, immediately **before** the second dose is given). **(3)**

(b) It is known that the level of serum in the body has to be continuously above 20 milligrams before the victim starts to confess. Find how many doses are needed before the captors should begin their interrogation. **(3)**

(c) Let u_n be the amount of serum (in milligrams) in his body just **after** his n^{th} dose. Show that $u_{n+1} = 0{\cdot}522u_n + 25$. **(1)**

(d) It is also known that 55 milligrams of this serum in the body will prove fatal, and the captors wish to keep Agent 004 alive. Is there any maximum length of time for which they can continue to administer this serum and still keep him alive? **(3)**

6. A builder has obtained a large supply of 4 metre rafters. He wishes to use them to build some holiday chalets. The planning department insists that the gable end of each chalet should be in the form of an isosceles triangle surmounting two squares, as shown in the diagram.

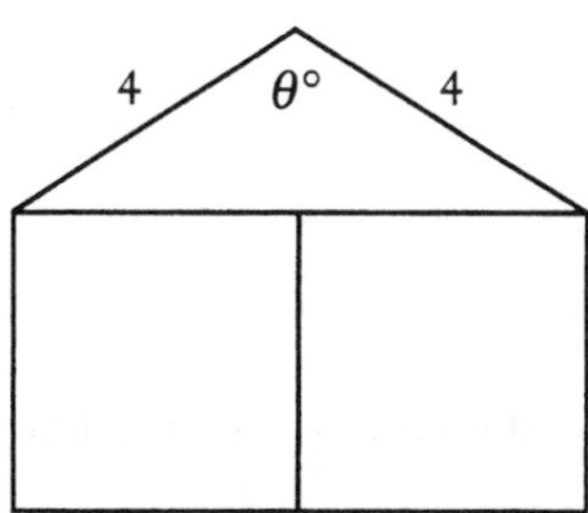

(a) If $\theta°$ is the angle shown in the diagram and A is the area (in square metres) of the gable end, show that

$$A = 8(2 + \sin\theta° - 2\cos\theta°).$$ **(4)**

(b) Express $8\sin\theta° - 16\cos\theta°$ in the form $k\sin(\theta - \alpha)°$. **(3)**

(c) Find algebraically the value of θ for which the area of the gable end is 30 square metres. **(4)**

Marks

7. When the switch in this circuit was closed, the computer printed out a graph of the current flowing (I microamps) against the time (t seconds). This graph is shown in figure 1.

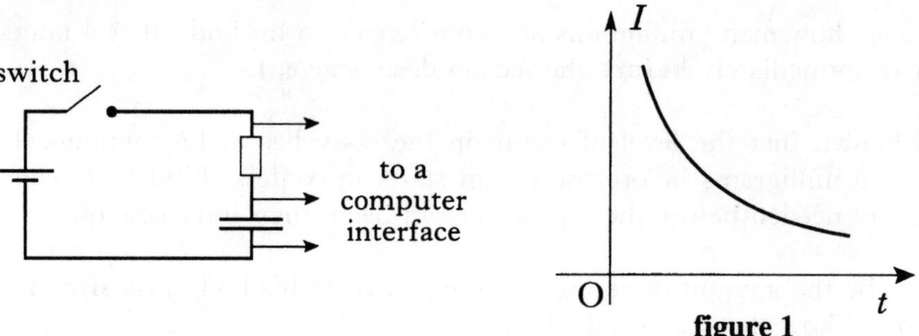

figure 1

In order to determine the equation of the graph shown in figure 1, values of $\log_e I$ were plotted against $\log_e t$ and the best fitting straight line was drawn as shown in figure 2.

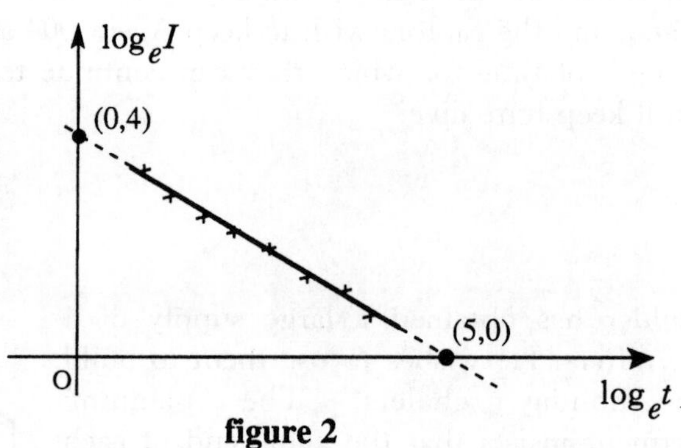

figure 2

(a) Find the equation of the line shown in figure 2 in terms of $\log_e I$ and $\log_e t$. **(2)**

(b) Hence or otherwise show that I and t satisfy a relationship of the form $I = kt^r$ stating the values of k and r. **(4)**

Marks

8. An oil production platform, $9\sqrt{3}$ km offshore, is to be connected by a pipeline to a refinery on shore, 100 km down the coast from the platform as shown in the diagram.

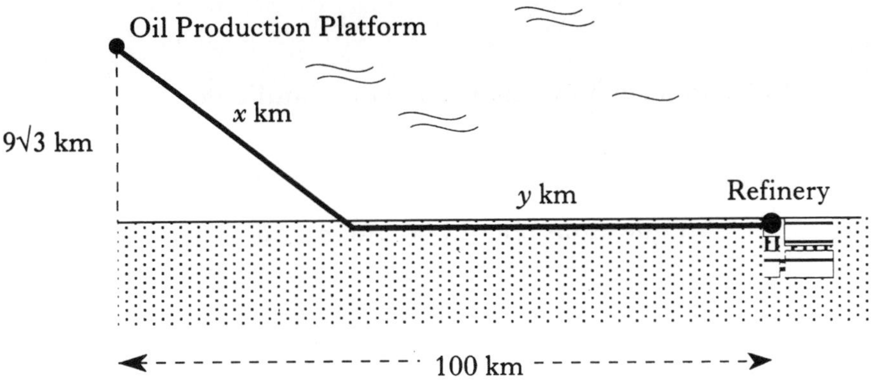

The length of underwater pipeline is x km and the length of pipeline on land is y km. It costs £2 million to lay each kilometre of pipeline underwater and £1 million to lay each kilometre of pipeline on land.

(a) Show that the total cost of this pipeline is £$C(x)$ million where

$$C(x) = 2x + 100 - \left(x^2 - 243\right)^{\frac{1}{2}}.$$ **(3)**

(b) Show that $x = 18$ gives a minimum cost for this pipeline.

Find this minimum cost and the corresponding total length of the pipeline. **(7)**

[END OF QUESTION PAPER]

NATIONAL QUALIFICATIONS

MODEL PAPER B

MATHEMATICS HIGHER

Paper 1
(Non-calculator)

Refer to page 3 for Instructions to Candidates

All questions should be attempted

Marks

1. Find $\int \left(3x^3 + 4x\right) dx.$ **(3)**

2.

R S T

Relative to the top of a hill, three gliders have positions given by R(–1, –8, –2), S(2, –5, 4) and T(3, –4, 6).

Prove that R, S and T are collinear. **(3)**

Marks

3. *(a)* $f(x) = 4x^2 - 3x + 5$.
Show that $f(x+1)$ simplifies to $4x^2 + 5x + 6$ and find a similar expression for $f(x-1)$.

Hence show that $\dfrac{f(x+1) - f(x-1)}{2}$ simplifies to $8x - 3$. **(3)**

(b) $g(x) = 2x^2 + 7x - 8$.

Find a similar expression for $\dfrac{g(x+1) - g(x-1)}{2}$. **(3)**

(c) By examining your answers for *(a)* and *(b)*, **write down** the simplified expression for $\dfrac{h(x+1) - h(x-1)}{2}$, where $h(x) = 3x^2 + 5x - 1$. **(1)**

4. If $\boldsymbol{u} = \begin{pmatrix} -3 \\ 3 \\ 3 \end{pmatrix}$ and $\boldsymbol{v} = \begin{pmatrix} 1 \\ 5 \\ -1 \end{pmatrix}$, write down the components of $\boldsymbol{u} + \boldsymbol{v}$ and $\boldsymbol{u} - \boldsymbol{v}$.

Hence show that $\boldsymbol{u} + \boldsymbol{v}$ and $\boldsymbol{u} - \boldsymbol{v}$ are perpendicular. **(3)**

5. The straight line $y = x$ cuts the circle $x^2 + y^2 - 6x - 2y - 24 = 0$ at A and B.

(a) Find the coordinates of A and B. **(3)**

(b) Find the equation of the circle which has AB as diameter. **(3)**

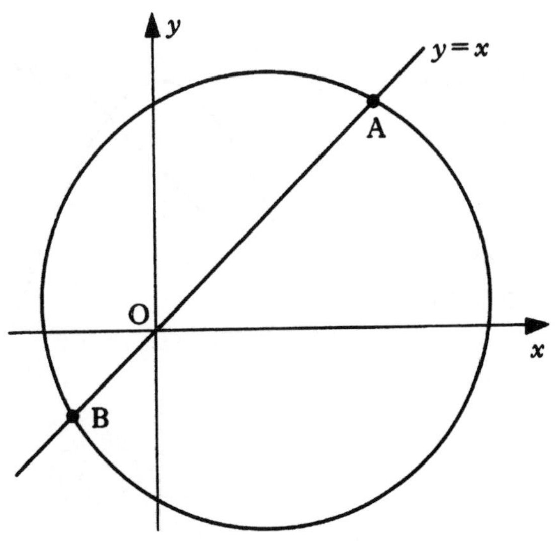

Marks

6. A sequence is defined by the recurrence relation

$$u_n = 0 \cdot 9u_{n-1} + 2, \qquad u_1 = 3$$

(a) Calculate the value of u_2. **(1)**

(b) What is the smallest value of n for which $u_n > 6$? **(1)**

(c) Find the limit of this sequence as $n \to \infty$. **(2)**

7. Show that $x^2 + 8x + 18$ can be written in the form $(x + a)^2 + b$.

Hence or otherwise find the coordinates of the turning point of the curve with equation $y = x^2 + 8x + 18$. **(4)**

8. If $\cos\theta = \frac{4}{5}$, $0 \le \theta < \frac{\pi}{2}$, find the **exact** value of

(a) $\sin 2\theta$ **(2)**

(b) $\sin 4\theta$. **(3)**

9. Find the gradient of the tangent to the parabola $y = \sqrt{3}\,x - x^2$ at (0, 0).

Hence calculate the size of the angle between the line $y = x$ and this tangent. **(6)**

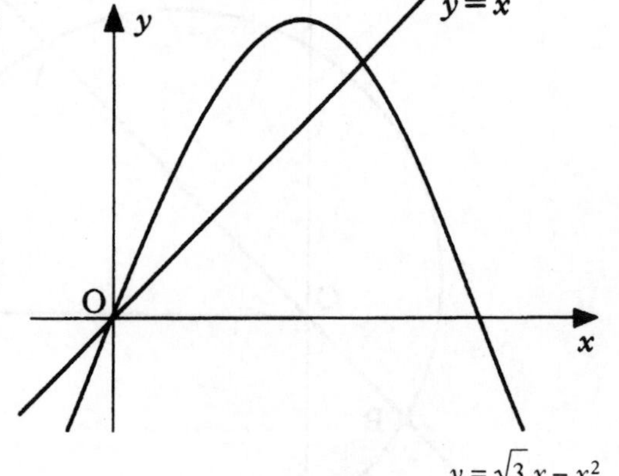

Marks

10.

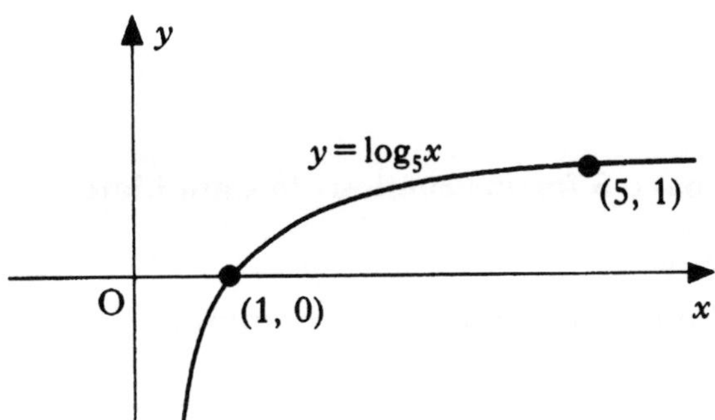

The diagram shows a sketch of part of the graph of $y = \log_5 x$.

(a) Make a copy of the graph of $y = \log_5 x$.

On your copy, sketch the graph of $y = \log_5 x + 1$.

Find the coordinates of the point where it crosses the x-axis. **(3)**

(b) Make a second copy of the graph of $y = \log_5 x$.

On your copy, sketch the graph of $y = \log_5 \frac{1}{x}$. **(2)**

11. Differentiate $\sin^3 x$ with respect to x.

Hence find $\int \sin^2 x \cos x \, dx$ **(4)**

[*END OF QUESTION PAPER*]

NATIONAL QUALIFICATIONS

MODEL PAPER B

MATHEMATICS
HIGHER
Paper 2

Refer to page 3 for Instructions to Candidates

All questions should be attempted

Marks

1. The graph of the curve with equation $y = 2x^3 + x^2 - 13x + a$ crosses the x-axis at the the point (2, 0).

(*a*) Find the value of a and hence write down the coordinates of the point at which this curve crosses the y-axis. **(3)**

(*b*) Find algebraically the coordinates of the other points at which the curve crosses the x-axis. **(2)**

2. ABCD is a square. A is the point with coordinates (3, 4) and ODC has equation $y = \frac{1}{2}x$.

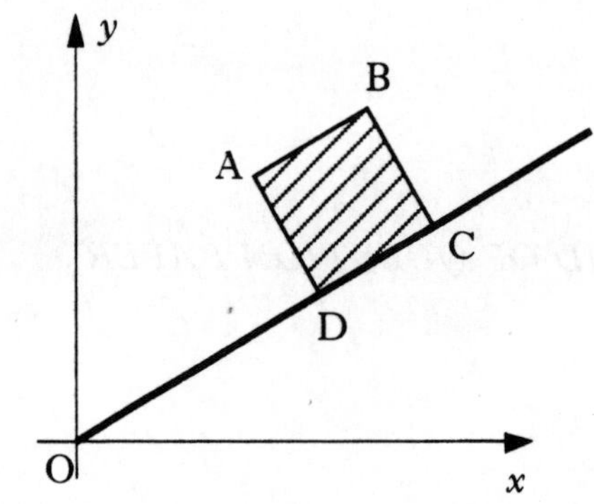

(*a*) Find the equation of the line AD. **(2)**

(*b*) Find the coordinates of D. **(3)**

(*c*) Find the area of the square ABCD. **(2)**

Marks

3.

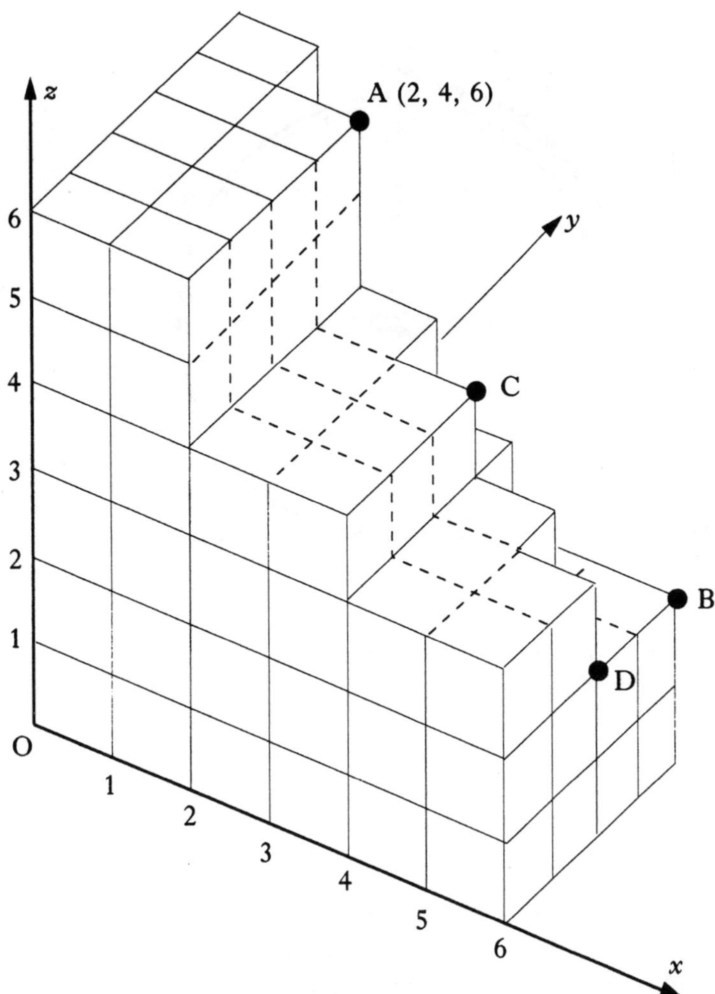

With coordinate axes as shown, the point A is (2, 4, 6).

(a) Write down the coordinates of B, C and D **(3)**

(b) Show that C is the midpoint of AD. **(1)**

(c) By using the components of the vectors $\overrightarrow{OA}$ and $\overrightarrow{OB}$, calculate the size of angle AOB, where O is the origin. **(3)**

(d) Hence calculate the size of angle OAB. **(1)**

Marks

4.

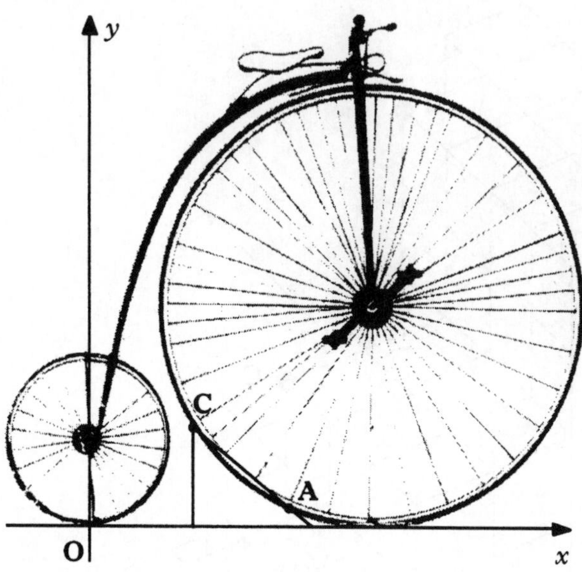

A penny-farthing bicycle on display in a museum is supported by a stand at points A and C. A and C lie on the front wheel.

With coordinate axes as shown and 1 unit = 5 cm, the equation of the rear wheel (the small wheel) is $x^2 + y^2 - 6y = 0$ and the equation of the front wheel is $x^2 + y^2 - 28x - 20y + 196 = 0$.

(a) (i) Find the distance between the centres of the two wheels.

(ii) Hence calculate the clearance, i.e., the smallest gap, between the front and rear wheels. Give your answer to the nearest millimetre. **(4)**

(b) B(7, 3) is half-way between A and C, and P is the centre of the front wheel.

(i) Find the gradient of PB.

(ii) Hence find the equation of AC and the coordinates of A and C. **(4)**

5. *(a)* Express $3\sin x° - \cos x°$ in the form $k\sin(x - \alpha)°$, where $k > 0$ and $0 \leq \alpha \leq 90$. **(3)**

(b) Hence find algebraically the values of x between 0 and 180 for which $3\sin x° - \cos x° = \sqrt{5}$. **(3)**

Marks

6. *(a)* For a particular radioactive substance, the mass m (in grams) at time t (in years) is given by

$$m = m_0 e^{-0{\cdot}02t}$$

where m_0 is the original mass.

If the original mass is 500 grams, find the mass after 10 years. **(1)**

(b) The half-life of any material is the time taken for half of the mass to decay.

Find the half-life of this substance. **(3)**

(c) Illustrate **all** of the above information on a graph. **(2)**

7. A yacht club is designing its new flag.

The flag is to consist of a red triangle on a yellow rectangular background.

In the yellow rectangle ABCD, AB measures 8 units and AD is 6 units. E and F lie on BC and CD, x units from B and C as shown in the diagram.

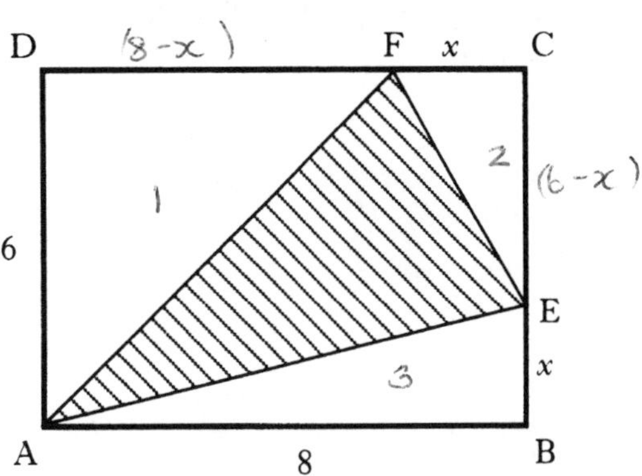

(a) Show that the area, H square units, of the red triangle AEF is given by
$H(x) = 24 - 4x + \frac{1}{2}x^2.$ **(3)**

(b) Hence find the greatest and least possible values of the area of traingle AEF. **(5)**

Marks

8. *(a)* The point A(2, 2) lies on the parabola $y = x^2 + px + q$.

Find a relationship between p and q. **(1)**

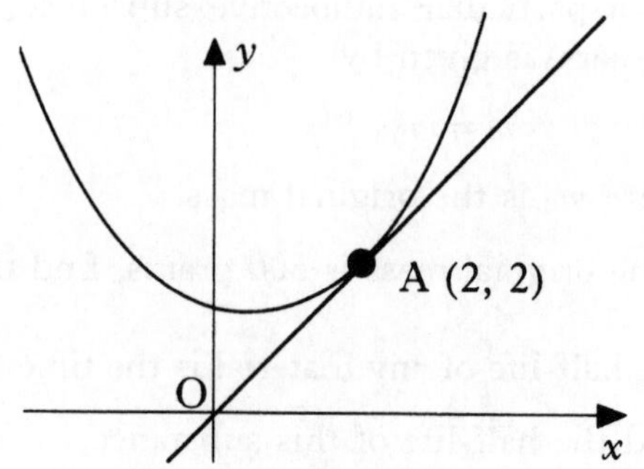

(b) The tangent to the parabola at A is the line $y = x$. Find the value of p. Hence find the equation of the parabola. **(3)**

(c) Using your answers for p and q, find the value of the discriminant of $x^2 + px + q = 0$. What feature of the above sketch is confirmed by this value? **(2)**

Marks

9. The cargo space of a small bulk carrier is 60 m long.

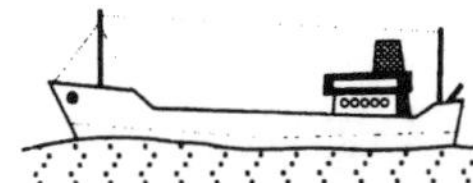

The shaded part of the diagram below represents the uniform cross-section of this space. It is shaped like the parabola with equation $y = \frac{1}{4}x^2$, $-6 \leq x \leq 6$, between the lines $y = 1$ and $y = 9$.

Find the area of this cross-section and hence find the volume of cargo that this ship can carry. **(6)**

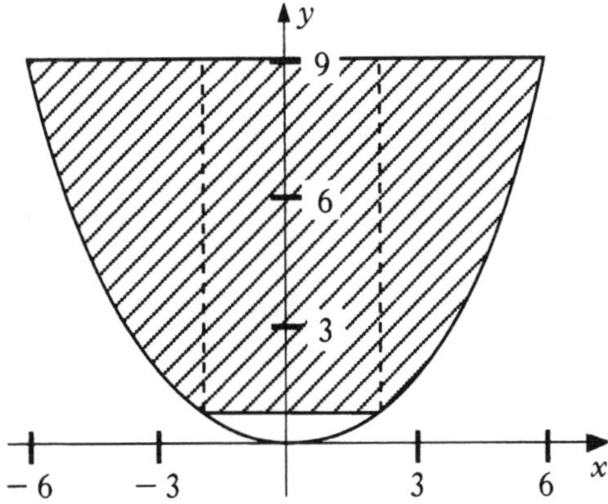

[END OF QUESTION PAPER]

NATIONAL QUALIFICATIONS

MODEL PAPER C

MATHEMATICS HIGHER

Paper 1

(Non-calculator)

Refer to page 3 for Instructions to Candidates

All questions should be attempted

Marks

1. (*a*) Show that $(x - 3)$ is a factor of $f(x)$, where $f(x) = 2x^3 + 3x^2 - 23x - 12$. **(2)**

(*b*) Hence express $f(x)$ in its fully factorised form. **(2)**

2. Find $\int (6x^2 - x + \cos x)\,dx$. **(4)**

3 A triangle ABC has vertices A(4, 8), B(1, 2) and C(7, 2).

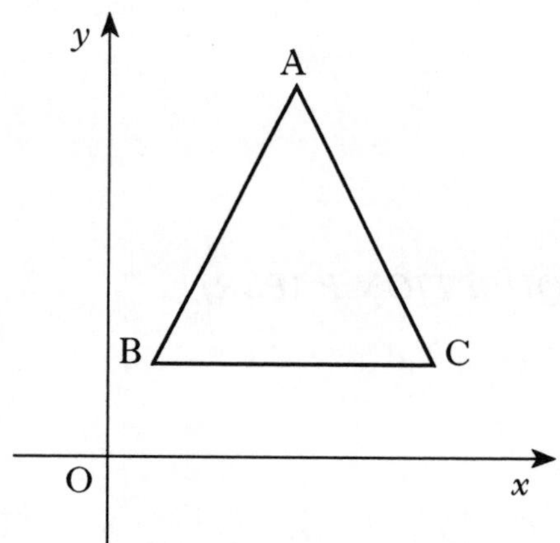

(*a*) Show that the triangle is isosceles. **(2)**

(*b*) (i) The altitudes AD and BE intersect at H, where D and E lie on BC and CA respectively. Find the coordinates of H. **(5)**

(ii) Hence show that H lies one quarter of the way up DA. **(1)**

Marks

4. Find $\frac{dy}{dx}$ where $y = \frac{4}{x^2} + x\sqrt{x}$. **(4)**

5. The functions f and g, defined on suitable domains, are given by

$$f(x) = \frac{1}{x^2 - 4} \text{ and } g(x) = 2x + 1.$$

(*a*) Find an expression for $h(x)$ where $h(x) = g(f(x))$. Give your answer as a single fraction. **(4)**

(*b*) State a suitable domain for h. **(1)**

6. Given that $\tan \alpha = \frac{\sqrt{11}}{3}$, $0 < \alpha < \frac{\pi}{2}$, find the exact value of $\sin 2\alpha$. **(4)**

7. The straight line shown in the diagram has equation $y = f(x)$. Determine $f'(x)$. **(2)**

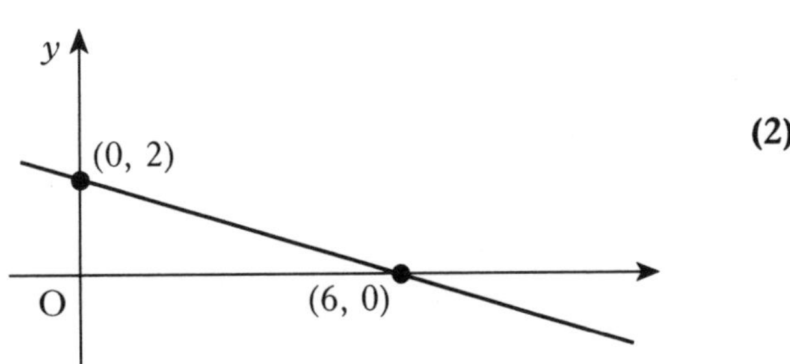

8. As shown in the diagram opposite, a set of experimental results gives a straight line graph when $\log_{10} y$ is plotted against $\log_{10} x$.

The straight line passes through (0, 1) and has a gradient of 2.

Express y in terms of x. **(5)**

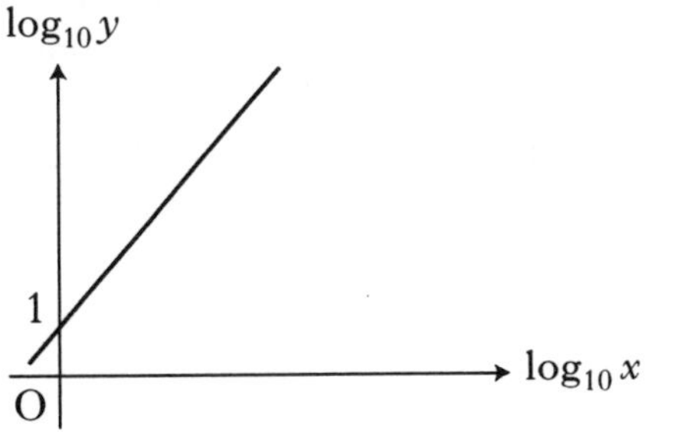

Marks

9. The diagram shows a sketch of the graph of $y = f(x)$, where $f(x) = a \log_2(x - b)$.
Find the values of a and b. **(2)**

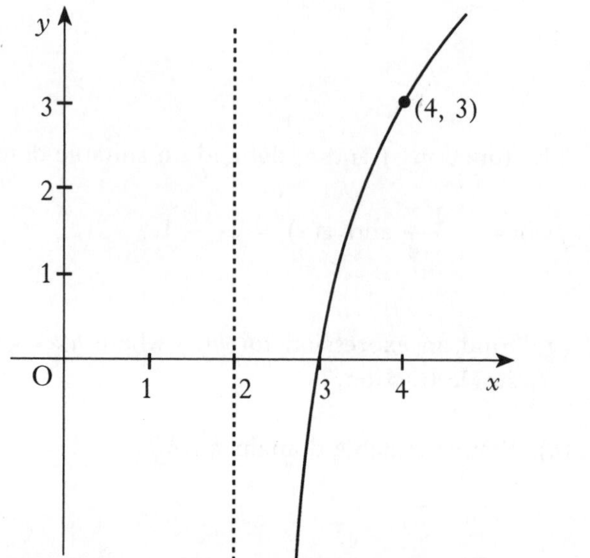

10. The roots of the equation $(x + 1)(x + k) = -4$ are equal.
Find the values of k. **(4)**

11. A ball is thrown vertically upwards. The height h metres of the ball t seconds after it is thrown, is given by the formula $h = 20t - 5t^2$.

(*a*) Find the speed of the ball when it is thrown (i.e. the rate of change of height with respect to time of the ball when it is thrown). **(2)**

(*b*) Find the speed of the ball after 2 seconds.
Explain your answer in terms of the movement of the ball. **(2)**

Marks

12. Solve the simultaneous equations

$k \sin x° = 2$

$k \cos x° = 2$ where $k > 0$ and $0 \leq x \leq 360$. **(4)**

[*END OF QUESTION PAPER*]

Refer to page 3 for Instructions to Candidates

All questions should be attempted

Marks

1. A Royal Navy submarine, exercising in the Firth of Clyde, is stationary on the seabed below a point S on the surface. S is the point (5, 4) as shown in the diagram.

A radar operator observes the frigate "Achilles" sailing in a straight line, passing through the points A_1 (−4, −1) and A_2 (−1, 1).

Similarly, the frigate "Belligerent" is observed sailing in a straight line, passing through the points B_1 (−7,−11) and B_2 (1, −1).

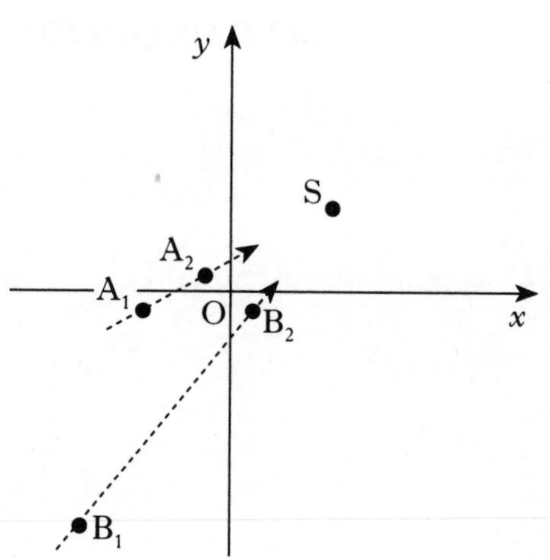

If both frigates continue to sail in straight lines, will either or both frigates pass directly over the submarine? **(4)**

Marks

2. The diagram shows a sketch of part of the graph of $y = x^3 - 2x^2 + x$.

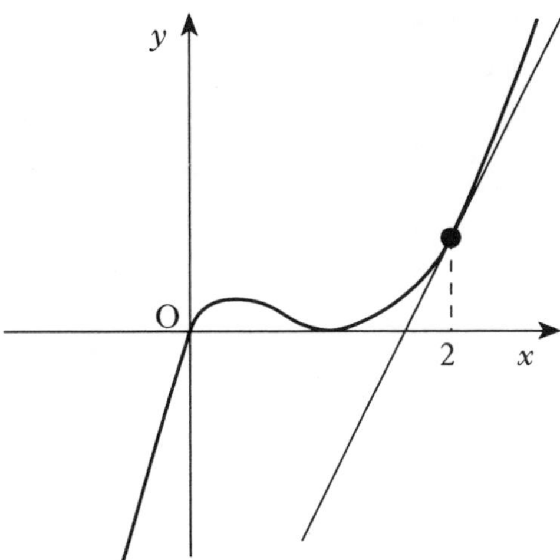

(a) Show that the equation of the tangent to the curve at $x = 2$ is $y = 5x - 8$. **(2)**

(b) Find algebraically the coordinates of the point where this tangent meets the curve again. **(3)**

3. Trees are sprayed weekly with the pesticide, "Killpest", whose manufacturers claim it will destroy 65% of all pests. Between the weekly sprayings, it is estimated that 500 new pests invade the trees.

A new pesticide, "Pestkill", comes onto the market. The manufacturers claim that it will destroy 85% of existing pests but it is estimated that 650 new pests per week will invade the trees.

Which pesticide will be more effective in the long term? **(5)**

Marks

4. (*a*) (i) Diagram 1 shows part of the graph of the function f defined by $f(x) = b \sin ax°$, where a and b are constants.

Write down the values of a and b.

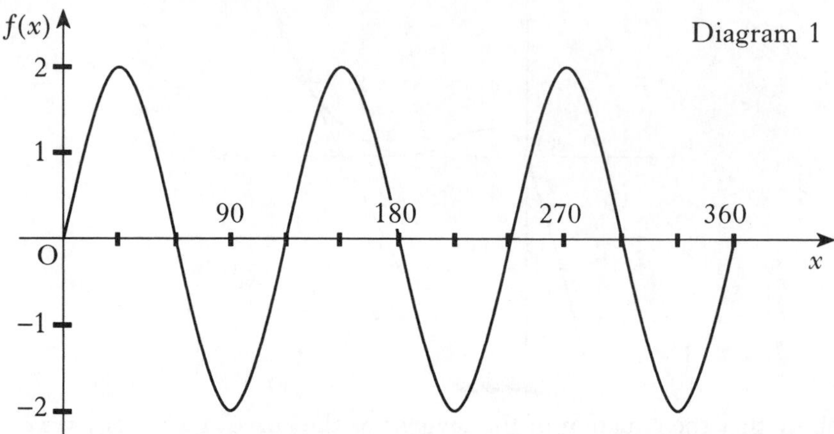

(ii) Diagram 2 shows part of the graph of the function g defined by $g(x) = d \cos cx°$, where c and d are constants.

Write down the values of c and d. **(4)**

Diagram 2

(*b*) The function h is defined by $h(x) = f(x) + g(x)$.

Show that $h(x)$ can be expressed in terms of a single trigonometric function of the form $q \sin(px + r)°$ and find the values of p, q and r. **(3)**

Marks

5. Relative to a suitable set of coordinate axes with a scale of 1 unit to 2 kilometres, the positions of a transmitter mast, ship, aircraft and satellite dish are shown in the diagram below.

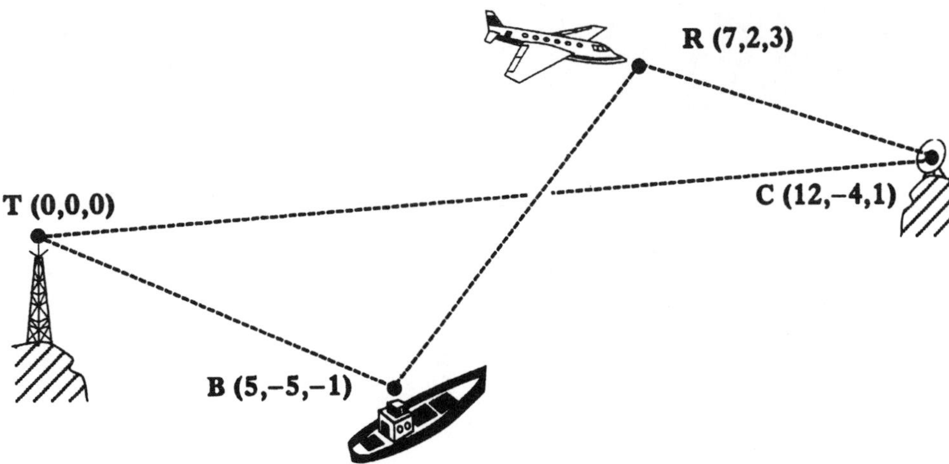

The top T of the transmitter mast is the origin, the bridge B on the ship is the point (5, –5, –1), the centre C of the dish on the top of a mountain is the point (12, –4, 1) and the reflector R on the aircraft is the point (7, 2, 3).

(a) Find the distance in kilometres from the bridge of the ship to the reflector on the aircraft. **(2)**

(b) Three minutes earlier, the aircraft was at the point M(–2, 4, 8·5). Find the speed of the aircraft in kilometres per hour. **(2)**

(c) Prove that the direction of the beam TC is perpendicular to the direction of the beam BR. **(3)**

(d) Calculate the size of angle TCR. **(3)**

Marks

6. The parabola $y = ax^2 + bx + c$ crosses the y-axis at (0, 3) and has two tangents drawn, as shown in the diagram.

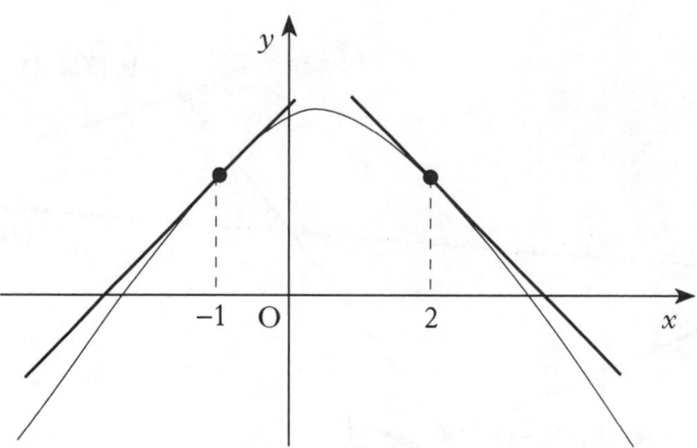

The tangent at $x = -1$ makes an angle of 45° with the positive direction of the x-axis and the tangent at $x = 2$ makes an angle of 135° with the positive direction of the x-axis.
Find the values of a, b and c. **(5)**

7. When newspapers were printed by lithograph, the newsprint had to run over three rollers, illustrated in the diagram by three circles. The centres A, B and C of the three circles are collinear.

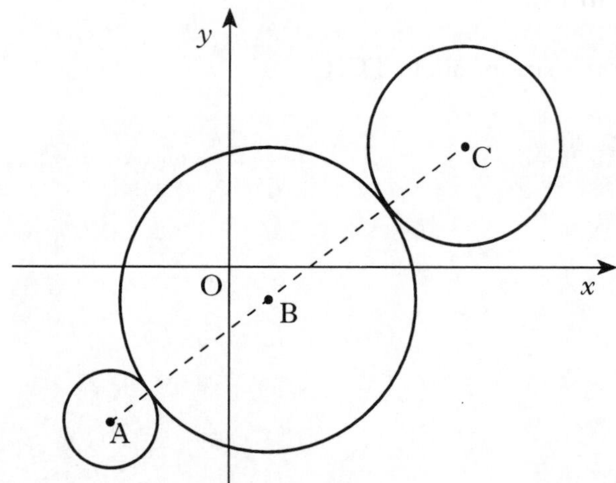

The equations of the circumferences of the outer circles are
$(x + 12)^2 + (y + 15)^2 = 25$ and $(x - 24)^2 + (y - 12)^2 = 100$.
Find the equation of the central circle. **(6)**

Marks

8. When building a road beside a vertical rockface, engineers often use wire mesh to cover the rockface. This helps to prevent rocks and debris from falling onto the road. The shaded region of the diagram below represents a part of such a rockface.

This shaded region is bounded by a parabola and a straight line.

The equation of the parabola is $y = 4 + \frac{5}{3}x - \frac{1}{6}x^2$ and the equation of the line is $y = 4 - \frac{1}{3}x$.

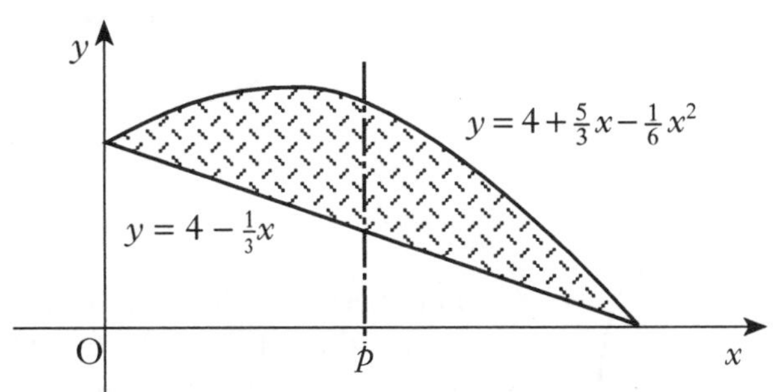

(*a*) Find algebraically the area of wire mesh required for this part of the rockface. **(4)**

(*b*) To help secure the wire mesh, weights are attached to the mesh along the line $x = p$ so that the area of mesh is bisected.

By using your answer to part (*a*), or otherwise, show that p satisfies the equation

$$p^3 - 18p^2 + 432 = 0.$$ **(2)**

(*c*) (i) Verify that $p = 6$ is a solution of this equation.

(ii) Find algebraically the other two solutions of this equation.

(iii) Explain why $p = 6$ is the only valid solution to this problem. **(4)**

Marks

9. Linktown Church is considering designs for a logo for their parish magazine. The "C" is part of a circle and the centre of the circle is the mid-point of the vertical arm of the "L". Since the "L" is clearly smaller than the "C", the designer wishes to ensure that the total length of the arms of the "L" is as long as possible.

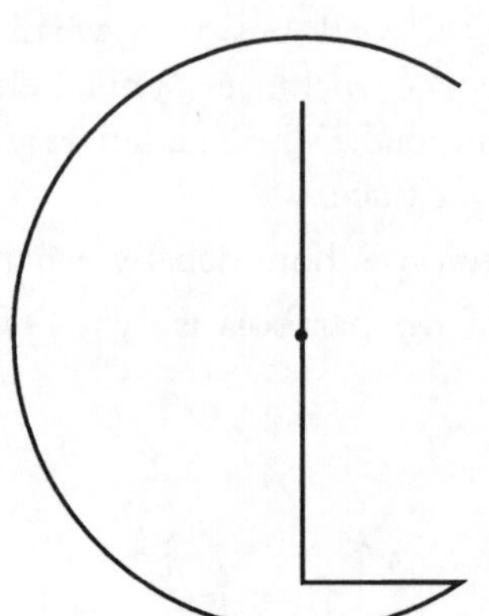

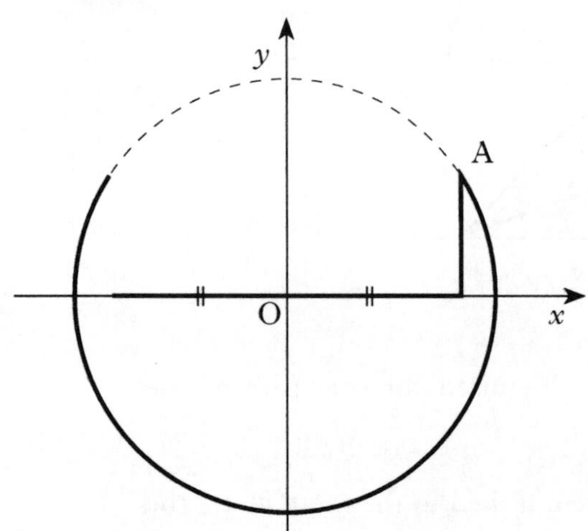

The designer decides to call the point where the "L" and "C" meet A and chooses to draw coordinate axes so that A is in the first quadrant. With axes as shown, the equation of the circle is $x^2 + y^2 = 20$.

(*a*) If A has coordinates (x,y), show that the total length T of the arms of the "L" is given by $T = 2x + \sqrt{20 - x^2}$. **(2)**

(*b*) Show that for a stationary value of T, x satisfies the equation

$$x = 2\sqrt{20 - x^2}.$$ **(3)**

(*c*) By squaring both sides, solve this equation.
Hence find the greatest length of the arms of the "L". **(3)**

[*END OF QUESTION PAPER*]

MODEL PAPER D

MATHEMATICS
HIGHER
Paper 1
(Non-calculator)

Refer to page 3 for Instructions to Candidates

All questions should be attempted

Marks

1. Find the equation of the tangent at the point (3, 4) on the circle

$$x^2 + y^2 + 2x - 4y - 15 = 0.$$ **(4)**

2. A is the point (2, –5, 6), B is (6, –3, 4) and C is (12, 0, 1). Show that A, B and C are collinear and determine the ratio in which B divides AC. **(3)**

3. Express $x^4 - x$ in its fully factorised form. **(3)**

Marks

4. Part of the graph of $y = f(x)$ is shown in the diagram. On separate diagrams, sketch the graphs of

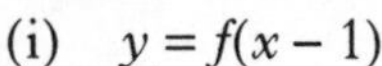

(i) $y = f(x - 1)$

(ii) $y = -f(x) - 2$

indicating on each graph the images of A, B, C and D. **(4)**

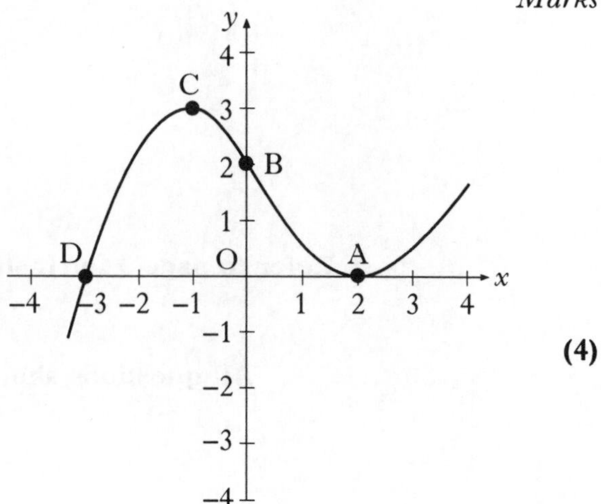

5. Find $f'(4)$ where $f(x) = \dfrac{x-1}{\sqrt{x}}$. **(4)**

6. A sequence is defined by the recurrence relation $u_{n+1} = 0{\cdot}3u_n + 5$ with first term u_1.

(*a*) Explain why this sequence has a limit as n tends to infinity. **(1)**

(*b*) Find the **exact** value of this limit. **(2)**

7. (*a*) $f(x) = 2x + 1$, $g(x) = x^2 + k$, where k is a constant.

(i) Find $g(f(x))$.

(ii) Find $f(g(x))$. **(2)**

(*b*) (i) Show that the equation $g(f(x)) - f(g(x)) = 0$ simplifies to $2x^2 + 4x - k = 0$.

(ii) Determine the nature of the roots of this equation when $k = 6$.

(iii) Find the value of k for which $2x^2 + 4x - k = 0$ has equal roots. **(7)**

Marks

8. The diagram shows two right-angled triangles ABD and BCD with AB = 7 cm, BC = 4 cm and CD = 3 cm. Angle DBC = $x°$ and angle ABD = $y°$.

Show that the exact value of

$\cos(x+y)°$ is $\dfrac{20-6\sqrt{6}}{35}$. **(3)**

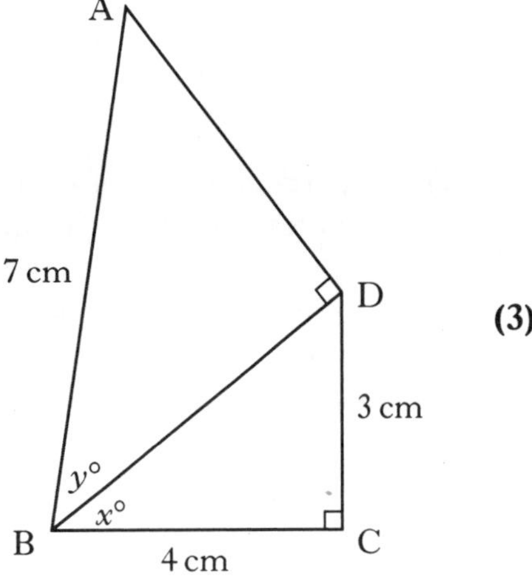

9. Find algebraically the values of x for which the function $f(x) = 2x^3 - 3x^2 - 36x$ is increasing. **(3)**

10. The framework of a child's swing has dimensions as shown in the diagram on the right.

Find the exact value of $\sin x°$. **(5)**

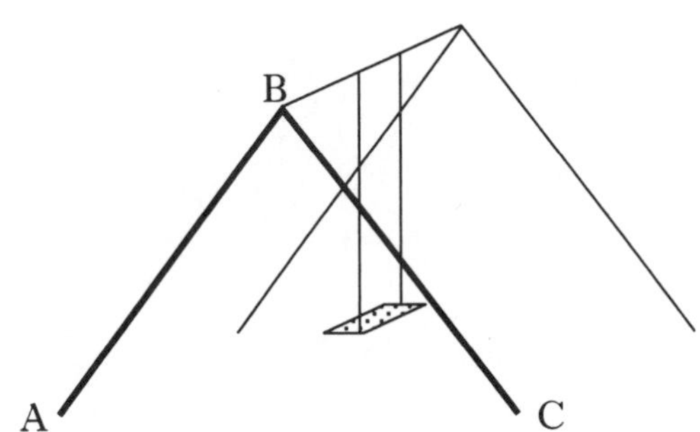

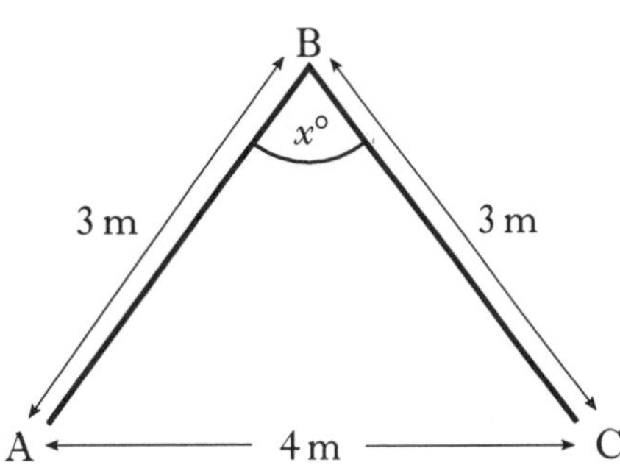

Marks

11. A mug of tea cools according to the law $T_t = T_0 10^{-kt}$, where T_0 is the initial temperature and T_t is the temperature after t minutes. All temperatures are in °C.

(*a*) A particular mug of tea cooled from boiling point (100 °C) to 10 °C in 10 minutes. Calculate the value of k. **(2)**

(*b*) By how many degrees will the temperature of this tea fall in the next 10 minutes? **(2)**

12. The line $y = -1$ is a tangent to a circle which passes through (0, 0) and (6, 0). Find the equation of this circle. **(5)**

[*END OF QUESTION PAPER*]

MODEL PAPER D

MATHEMATICS
HIGHER
Paper 2

Refer to page 3 for Instructions to Candidates

All questions should be attempted

Marks

1. A curve has equation $y = x^4 - 4x^3 + 3$.

(*a*) Find algebraically the coordinates of the stationary points. **(4)**

(*b*) Determine the nature of the stationary points. **(2)**

2. A triangle ABC has vertices A(–3, –3), B(–1, 1) and C(7, –3).

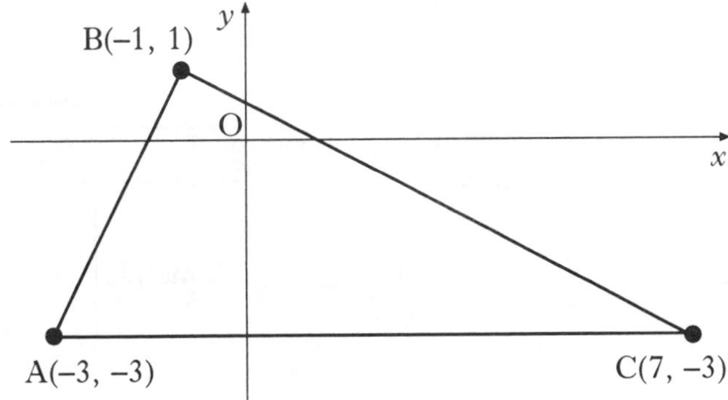

(*a*) Show that the triangle ABC is right-angled at B. **(3)**

(*b*) The medians AD and BE intersect at M.

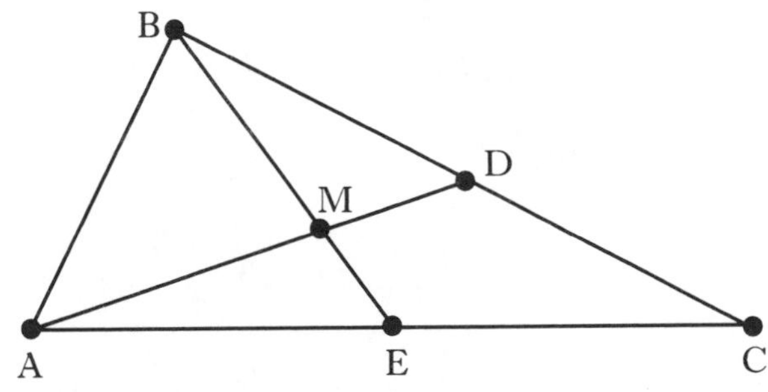

(i) Find the equations of AD and BE.

(ii) Hence find the coordinates of M. **(6)**

Marks

3. The first four levels of a stepped pyramid with a square base are shown in the diagram.

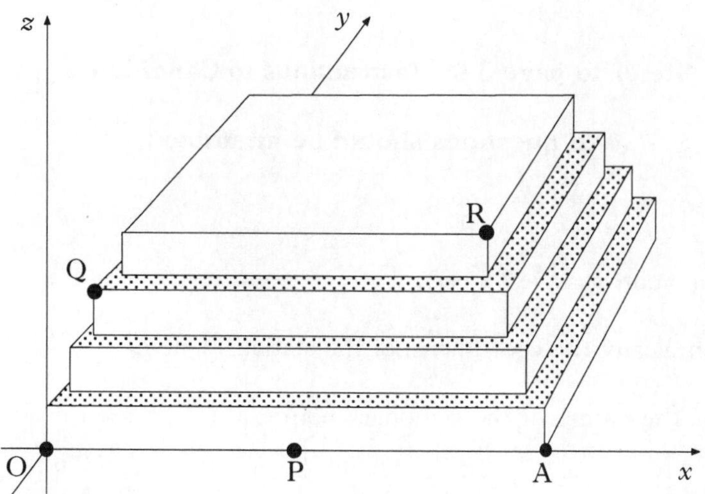

Each level is a square-based cuboid with a height of 3 m. The shaded parts indicate the steps which have a "width" of 1 m.

The height and "width" of a step at a corner are shown in this enlargement.

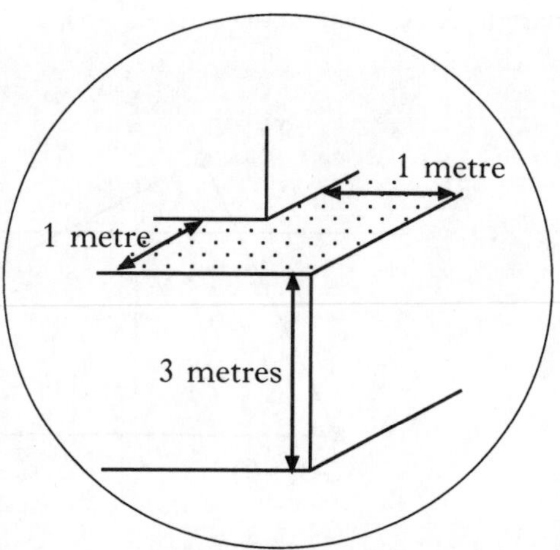

With coordinate axes as shown and 1 unit representing 1 metre, the coordinates of P and A are (12, 0, 0) and (24, 0, 0).

(*a*) Find the coordinates of Q and R. **(2)**

(*b*) Find the size of angle QPR. **(3)**

Marks

4. An artist has designed a "bow" shape which he finds can be modelled by the shaded area below. Calculate the area of this shape. **(5)**

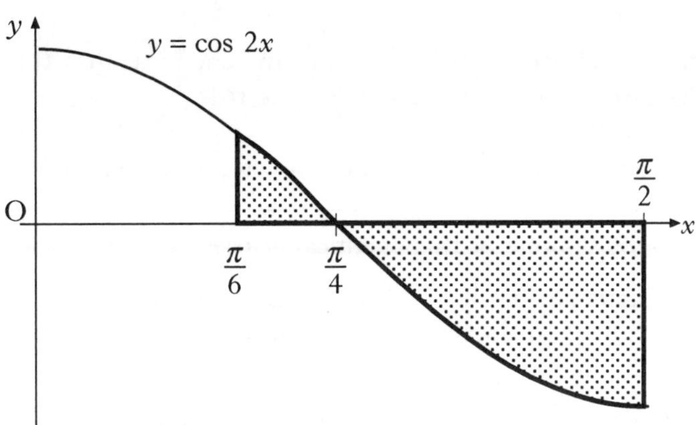

Marks

5. Biologists calculate that, when the concentration of a particular chemical in a sea loch reaches 5 milligrams per litre (mg/l), the level of pollution endangers the life of the fish.

A factory wishes to release waste containing this chemical into the loch. It is claimed that the discharge will not endanger the fish.

The Local Authority is supplied with the following information:

1. The loch contains none of this chemical at present.
2. The factory manager has applied to discharge waste once per week which will result in an increase in concentration of 2·5 mg/l of the chemical in the loch.
3. The natural tidal action will remove 40% of the chemical from the loch every week.

(a) Show that this level of discharge would result in fish being endangered. **(3)**

When this result is announced, the company agrees to install a cleaning process that reduces the concentration of chemical released into the loch by 30%.

(b) Show the calculations you would use to check this revised application.

Should the Local Authority grant permission? **(3)**

Marks

6. *(a)* Solve the equation $3\sin 2x° = 2\sin x°$ for $0 \leq x \leq 360$. **(4)**

(b) The diagram below shows parts of the graphs of sine functions f and g.
State expressions for $f(x)$ and $g(x)$. **(1)**

(c) Use your answers to part *(a)* to find the coordinates of A and B. **(2)**

(d) Hence state the values of x in the interval $0 \leq x \leq 360$ for which $3\sin 2x° < 2\sin x°$. **(2)**

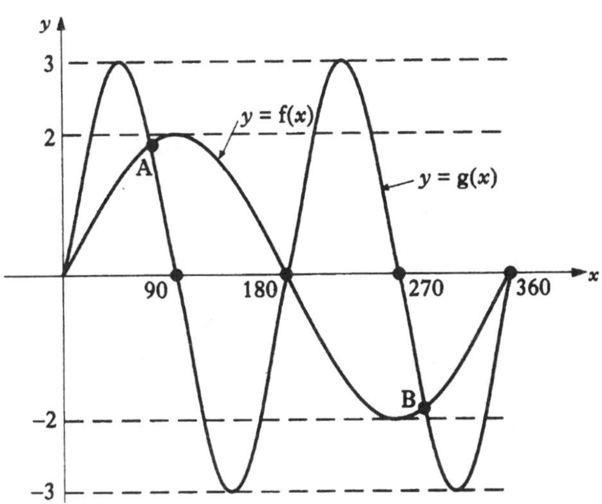

Marks

7.

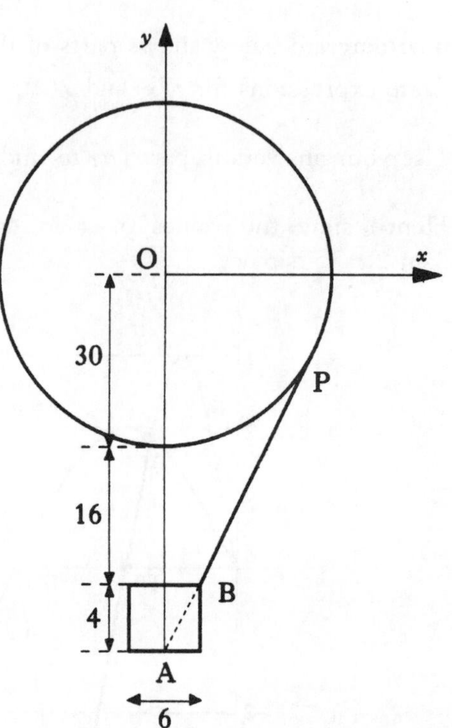

A spherical hot-air balloon has radius 30 feet. Cables join the balloon to the gondola which is cylindrical with diameter 6 feet and height 4 feet. The top of the gondola is 16 feet below the bottom of the balloon.

Coordinate axes are chosen as shown in the diagram. One of the cables is represented by PB and PBA is a straight line.

(a) Find the equation of the cable PB. **(3)**

(b) State the equation of the circle representing the balloon. **(1)**

(c) Prove that this cable is a tangent to the balloon and find the coordinates of the point P. **(4)**

Marks

8. An artist has been asked to design a window made from pieces of coloured glass with different shapes. To preserve a balance of colour, each shape must have the **same** area. Three of the shapes used are drawn below.

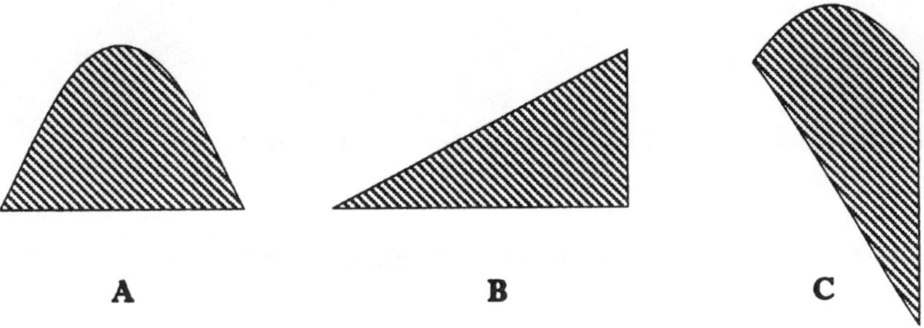

Relative to x, y-axes, the shapes are positioned as shown below. The artist drew the curves accurately by using the equation(s) shown in each diagram.

(a) Find the area shaded under $y = 2x - x^2$. **(2)**

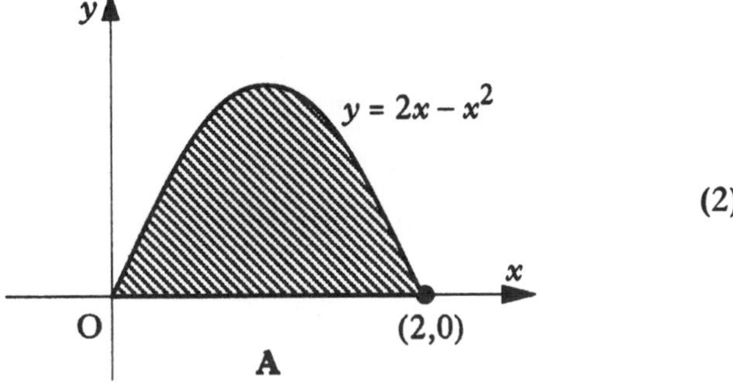

(b) Use the area found in part *(a)* to find the value of p. **(2)**

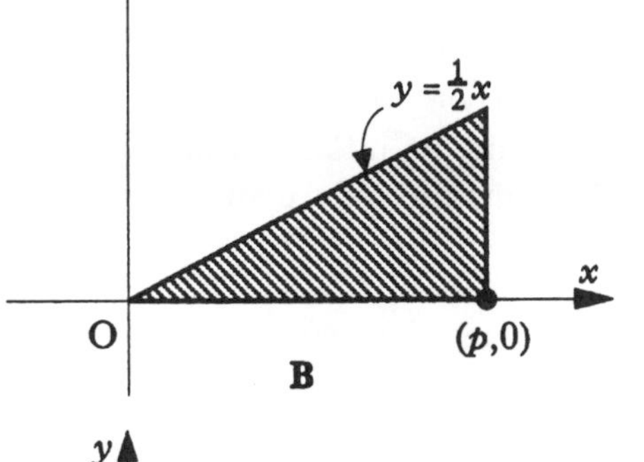

(c) Prove that q satisfies the equation $\cos q + \sin q = 0{\cdot}081$ and hence find the value of q to 2 significant figures. **(8)**

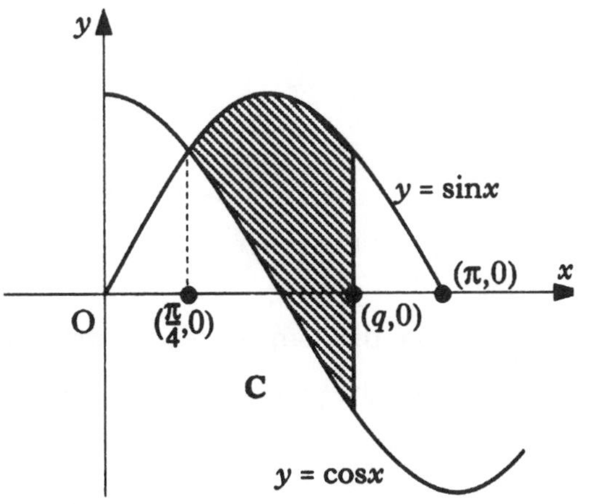

[END OF QUESTION PAPER]

NATIONAL
QUALIFICATIONS

MODEL PAPER E

MATHEMATICS
HIGHER
Paper 1
(Non-calculator)

Refer to page 3 for Instructions to Candidates

All questions should be attempted

Marks

1. In the diagram, A is the point (7, 0).

B is (–3, –2) and C is (–1, 8).

The median CE and the altitude BD intersect at J.

(a) Find the equations of CE and BD.

(b) Find the coordinates of J. **(5)**

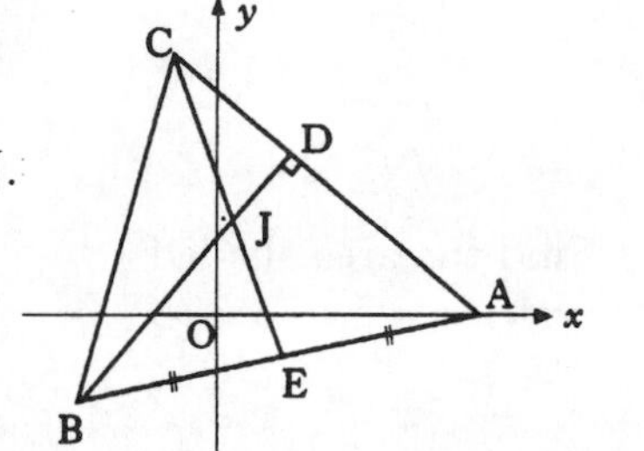

2. The diagram shows a sketch of part of the graph of $y = f(x)$. The graph has a point of inflection at $(0, a)$ and a maximum turning point at (b, c).

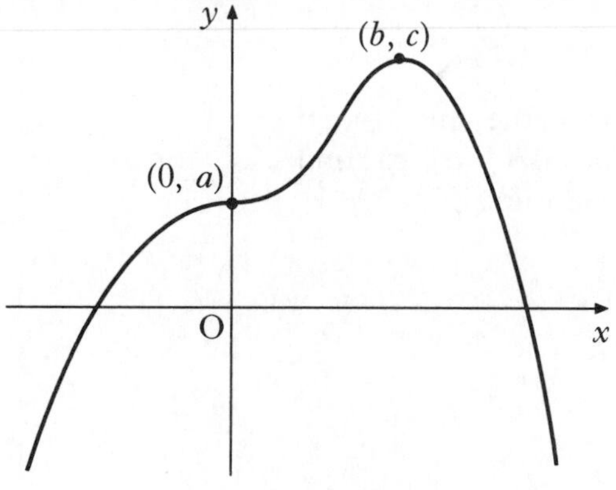

(*a*) Make a copy of this diagram and on it sketch the graph of $y = g(x)$ where $g(x) = f(x) + 1$. **(1)**

(*b*) On a separate diagram, sketch the graph of $y = f'(x)$. **(1)**

(*c*) Describe how the graph of $y = g'(x)$ is related to the graph of $y = f'(x)$. **(1)**

Marks

3. Part of the graph of $y = 5\log_{10}(2x + 10)$ is shown in the diagram (not to scale). This graph crosses the x-axis at the point A and the straight line $y = 10$ at the point B.

Find algebraically the x-coordinates of A and B. **(3)**

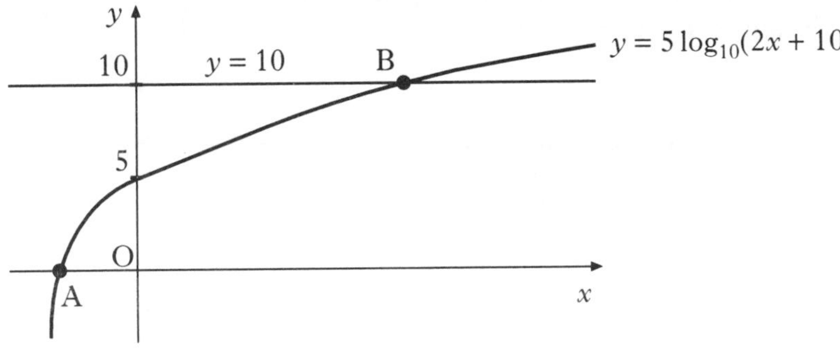

4. The diagram below shows a parabola with equation $y = 4x^2 + 3x - 5$ and a straight line with equation $5x + y + 12 = 0$.

A tangent to the parabola is drawn parallel to the given straight line.

Find the x-coordinate of the point of contact of this tangent. **(5)**

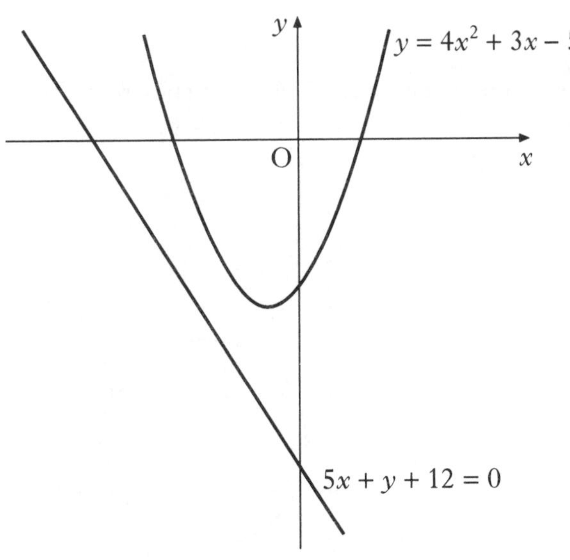

Marks

5. A ship is sailing due north at a constant speed. When at position A, a lighthouse L is observed on a bearing of $a°$. One hour later, when the ship is at position B, the lighthouse is on a bearing of $b°$.

The shortest distance between the ship and lighthouse during this hour was d miles.

(a) Prove that $\text{AB} = \dfrac{d}{\tan a°} - \dfrac{d}{\tan b°}$. **(2)**

(b) Hence prove that $\text{AB} = \dfrac{d\sin(b-a)°}{\sin a° \sin b°}$. **(2)**

6. Given that $y = 2x^2 + x$, find $\dfrac{dy}{dx}$ and hence show that $x\left(1+\dfrac{dy}{dx}\right) = 2y$. **(3)**

7. The curve $y = f(x)$ passes through the point $\left(\dfrac{\pi}{12}, 1\right)$ and $f'(x) = \cos 2x$.
Find $f(x)$. **(3)**

8. Two identical circles touch at the point P (9, 3) as shown in the diagram. One of the circles has equation $x^2 + y^2 - 10x - 4y + 12 = 0$.
Find the equation of the other circle. **(4)**

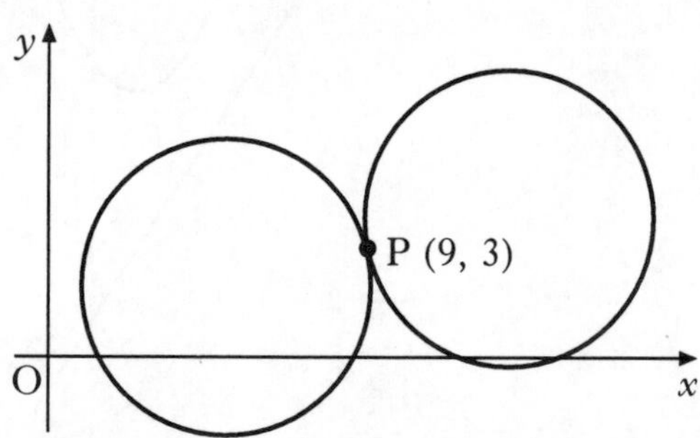

Marks

9. PQR is an equilateral triangle of side 2 units.

$\overrightarrow{PQ} = \boldsymbol{a}$, $\overrightarrow{PR} = \boldsymbol{b}$ and $\overrightarrow{QR} = \boldsymbol{c}$.

Evaluate $\boldsymbol{a}.(\boldsymbol{b} + \boldsymbol{c})$ and hence identify two vectors which are perpendicular. **(4)**

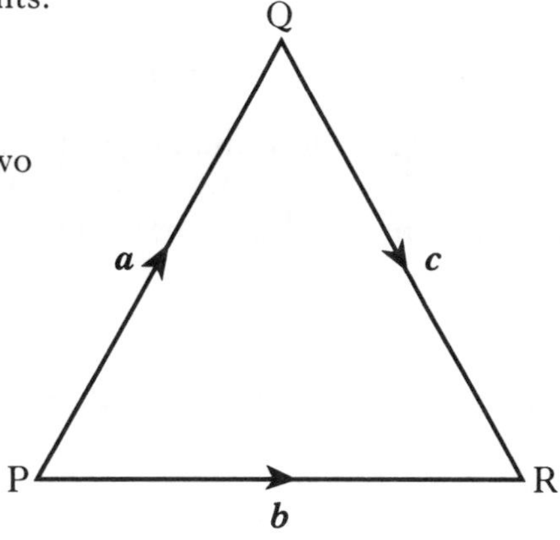

10. Diagram 1 shows 5 cars travelling up an incline on a roller-coaster. Part of the roller-coaster rail follows the curve with equation $y = 8 + 4\cos\frac{1}{2}x$.

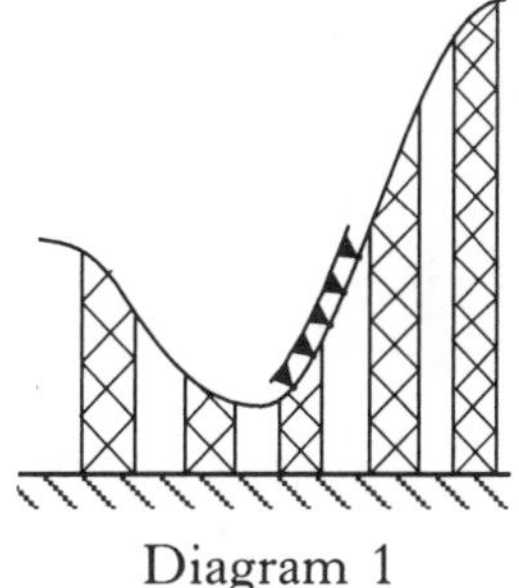

Diagram 1

Diagram 2 shows an enlargement of the last car and its position relative to a suitable set of axes. The floor of the car lies parallel to the tangent at P, the point of contact.

Calculate the acute angle a between the floor of the car and the horizontal when the car is at the point where $x_p = \frac{7\pi}{3}$.

Express your answer in degrees. **(4)**

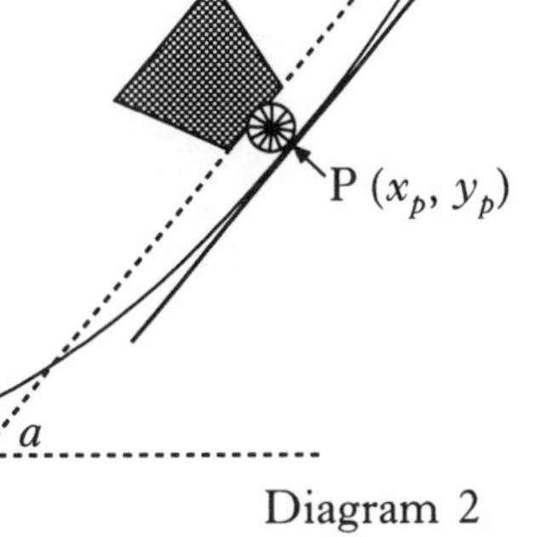

Diagram 2

Marks

11. (*a*) A sketch of part of the graph of $y = \frac{1}{x}$ is shown in the diagram.

The tangent at $A\left(a, \frac{1}{a}\right)$ has been drawn.

Find the gradient of this tangent. **(2)**

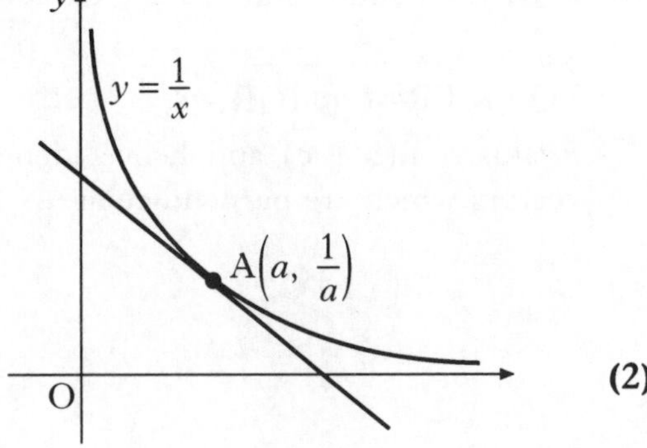

(*b*) Hence show that the equation of this tangent is $x + a^2y = 2a$. **(2)**

(*c*) This tangent cuts the y-axis at B and the x-axis at C.

(i) Calculate the area of triangle OBC.

(ii) Comment on your answer to *c*(i). **(4)**

12. Calculate the least positive integer value of k so that the graph of $y = kx^2 - 8x + k$ does not cut or touch the x-axis. **(4)**

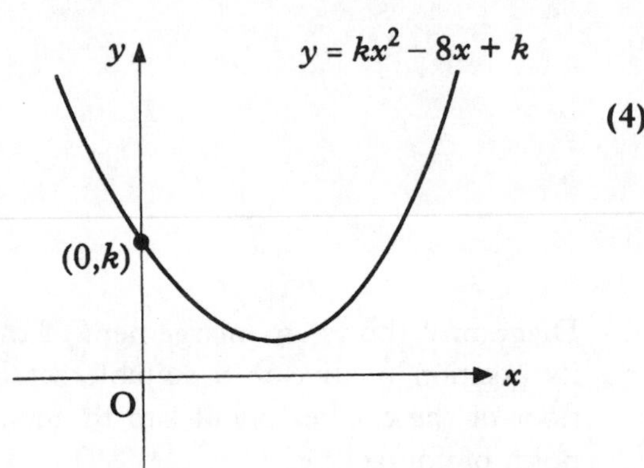

[END OF QUESTION PAPER]

Refer to page 3 for Instructions to Candidates

All questions should be attempted. *Marks*

1. *(a)* Find k if $x - 2$ is a factor of $x^3 + kx^2 - 4x - 12$. **(2)**

   (b) Hence express $f(x)$ in its fully factorised form. **(2)**

2. Diagram 1 shows a circle with equation $x^2 + y^2 + 10x - 2y - 14 = 0$ and a straight line, l_1, with equation $y = 2x + 1$.

   The line intersects the circle at A and B.

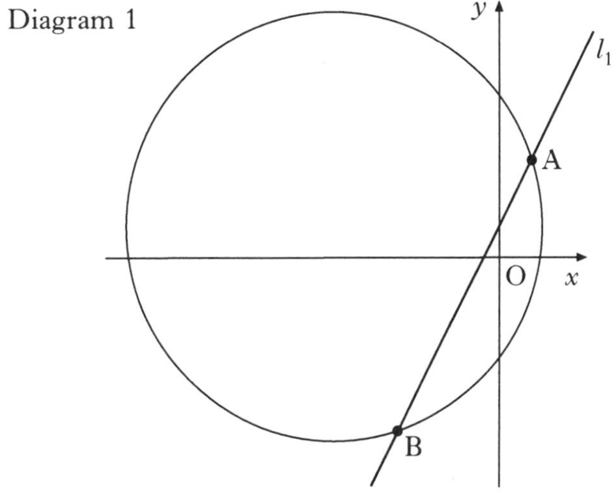

   (*a*) Find the coordinates of the points A and B. **(4)**

   (*b*) Diagram 2 shows a second line, l_2, which passes through the centre of the circle, C, and is at right angles to line l_1.

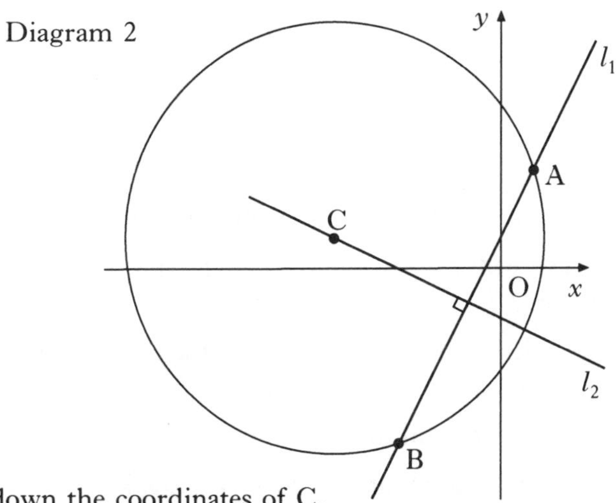

   (i) Write down the coordinates of C.

   (ii) Find the equation of the line l_2. **(4)**

Marks

3. Relative to the axes shown and with an appropriate scale, P(–1, 3, 2) and Q(5, 0, 5) represent points on a road. The road is then extended to the point R such that $\overrightarrow{PR} = \frac{4}{3}\overrightarrow{PQ}$.

(*a*) Find the coordinates of R. **(2)**

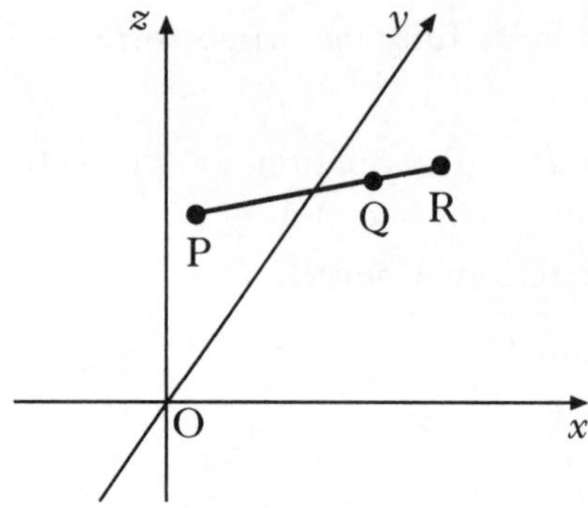

(*b*) Roads from P and R are built to meet at the point S (–2, 2, 5). Calculate the size of angle PSR. **(4)**

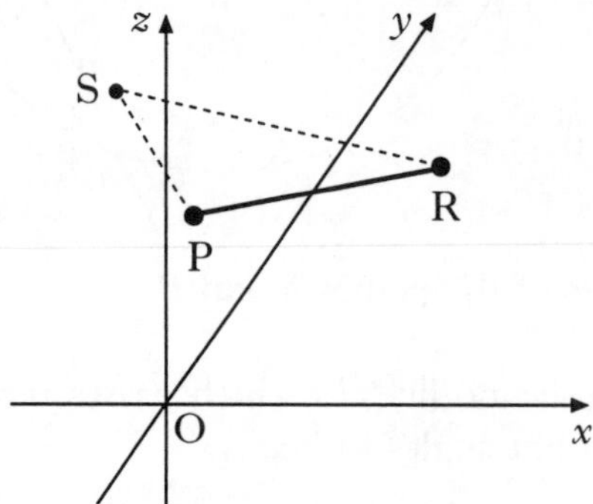

4. The sum of £1000 is placed in an investment account on January 1st and, thereafter, £100 is placed in the account on the first day of each month.

- Interest at the rate of 0·5% per month is credited to the account on the last day of each month.
- This interest is calculated on the amount in the account on the first day of the month.

(*a*) How much is in the account on June 30th? **(2)**

(*b*) On what date does the account first exceed £2000? **(2)**

(*c*) Find a recurrence relation which describes the amount in the account, explaining your notation carefully. **(2)**

Marks

5. *(a)* Express $\sin x° - 3\cos x°$ in the form $k\sin(x - \alpha)°$ where $k > 0$ and $0 \leq \alpha < 360$. Find the values of k and α. **(3)**

(b) Find the maximum value of $5 + \sin x° - 3\cos x°$ and state a value of x for which this maximum occurs. **(2)**

6. Diagram 1 shows a sketch of part of the graph of $y = f(x)$ where $f(x) = (x - 2)^2 + 1$.

The graph cuts the y-axis at A and has a minimum turning point at B.

(a) Write down the coordinates of A and B. **(2)**

Diagram 1

(b) Diagram 2 shows the graphs of $y = f(x)$ and $y = g(x)$ where $g(x) = 5 + 4x - x^2$.

Find the area enclosed by the two curves. **(3)**

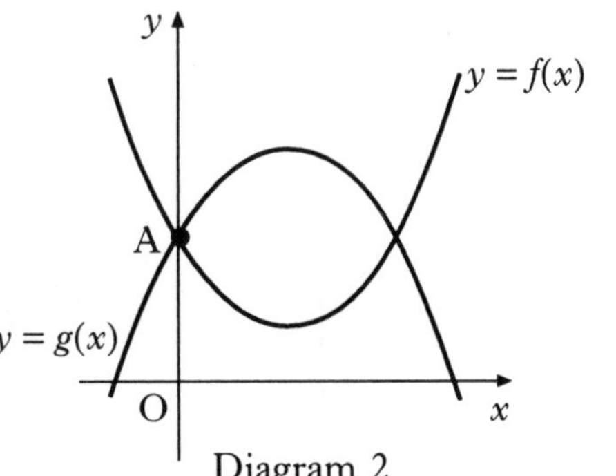

Diagram 2

(c) $g(x)$ can be written in the form $m + n \times f(x)$ where m and n are constants.

Write down the values of m and n. **(2)**

Marks

7. The radioactive element carbon-14 is sometimes used to estimate the age of organic remains such as bones, charcoal and seeds.

Carbon-14 decays according to a law of the form $y = y_0e^{kt}$ where y is the amount of radioactive nuclei present at time t years and y_0 is the initial amount of radioactive nuclei.

(*a*) The half-life of carbon-14, ie the time taken for half the radioactive nuclei to decay, is 5700 years. Find the value of the constant k, correct to 3 significant figures. **(3)**

(*b*) What percentage of the carbon-14 in a sample of charcoal will remain after 1000 years? **(3)**

8. The sketch represents part of the graph of a trigonometric function of the form $y = p\sin(x + r)° + q$. It crosses the axes at $(0, s)$ and $(t, 0)$, and has turning points at $(50, -2)$ and $(u, 4)$.

(*a*) Write down values for p, q, r and u. **(4)**

(*b*) Find the values for s and t. **(2)**

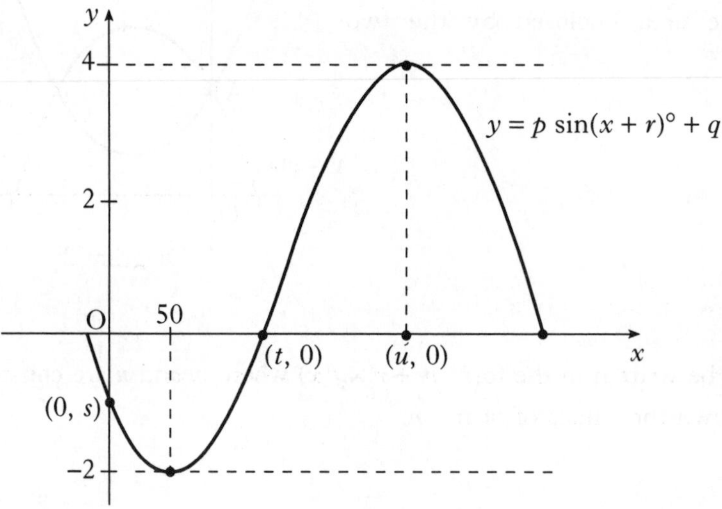

9. (*a*) Evaluate $\int_0^{\pi/2} \cos 2x \, dx$. **(2)**

(*b*) Draw a sketch and explain your answer **(2)**

Marks

10. A cuboid is to be cut out of a right square-based pyramid. The pyramid has a square base of side 8 cm and a vertical height of 10 cm.

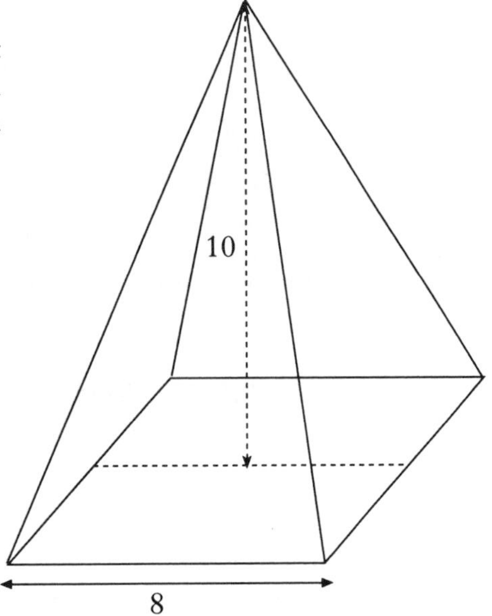

(*a*) The cuboid has a square base of side $2x$ cm and a height of h cm.

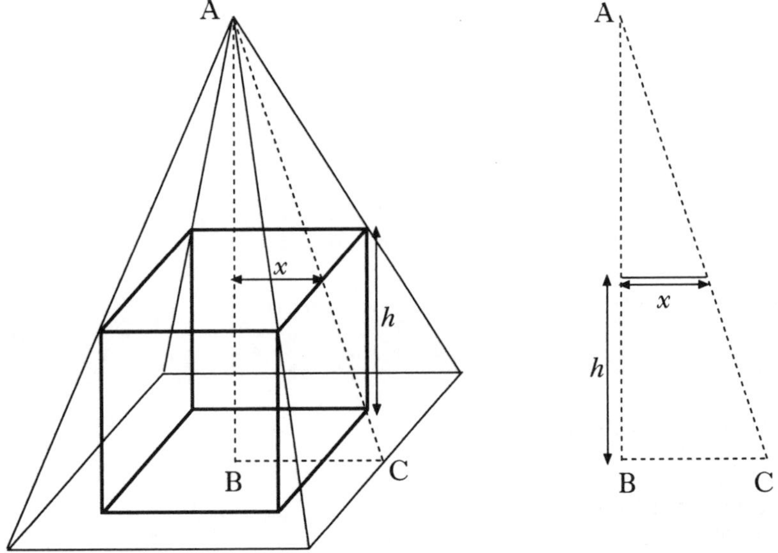

If the cuboid is to fit into the pyramid, use the information shown in triangle ABC, or otherwise, to show that:

(i) $h = 10 - \frac{5}{2}x$;

(ii) the volume, V, of the cuboid is given by $V = 40x^2 - 10x^3$. **(4)**

(*b*) Hence, find the dimensions of the square-based cuboid with the greatest volume which can be cut from the pyramid. **(4)**

[END OF QUESTION PAPER]

NATIONAL QUALIFICATIONS

MODEL PAPER F

MATHEMATICS
HIGHER
Paper 1
(Non-calculator)

Refer to page 3 for Instructions to Candidates

All questions should be attempted

Marks

1. A triangle ABC has vertices A(4, 3), B(6, 1) and C(–2, –3) as shown in the diagram. Find the equation of AM, the median from A. **(3)**

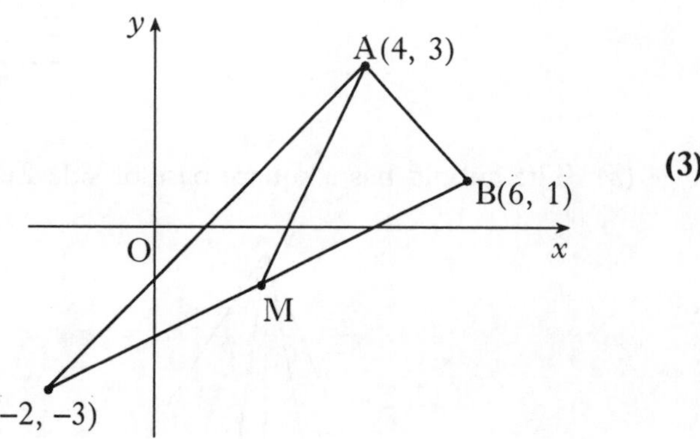

2. Express $x^3 - 4x^2 - 7x + 10$ in its fully factorised form. **(3)**

3. The circle shown has equation $(x - 3)^2 + (y + 2)^2 = 25$.

   Find the equation of the tangent at the point (6, 2). **(3)**

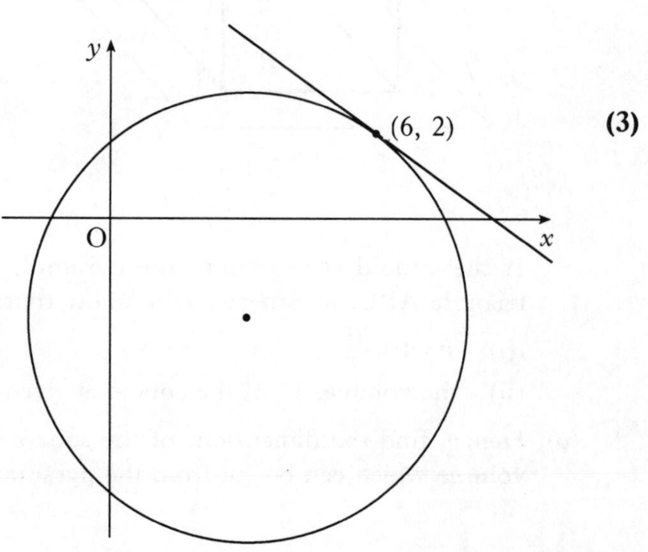

Marks

4. The map shows part of the coast road from Achnatruim to Inveranavan. In order to avoid the hairpin bends, it is proposed to build a straight causeway, as shown, with the southern end tangential to the existing road.

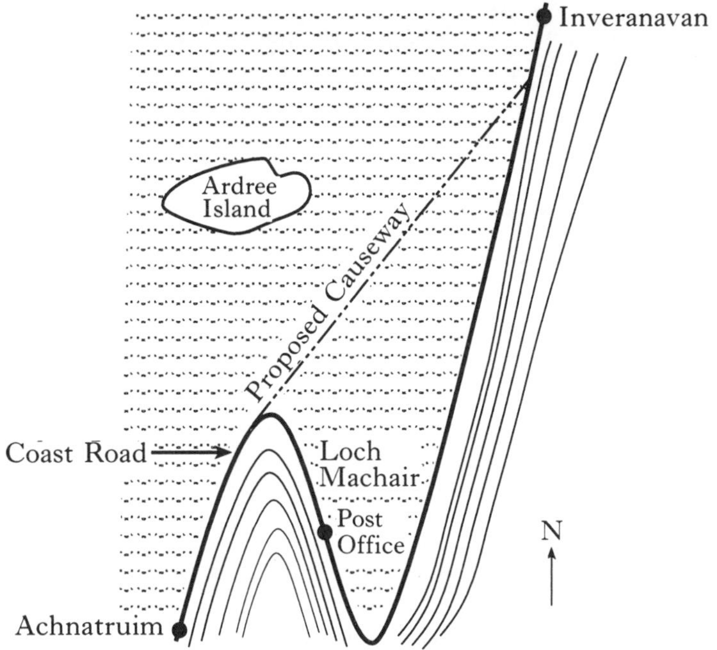

With the origin taken at the Post Office, the part of the coast road shown lies along the curve with equation $y = x^3 - 9x$. The causeway is represented by the line AB. The southern end of the proposed causeway is at the point A where $x = -2$, and the line AB is a tangent to the curve at A.

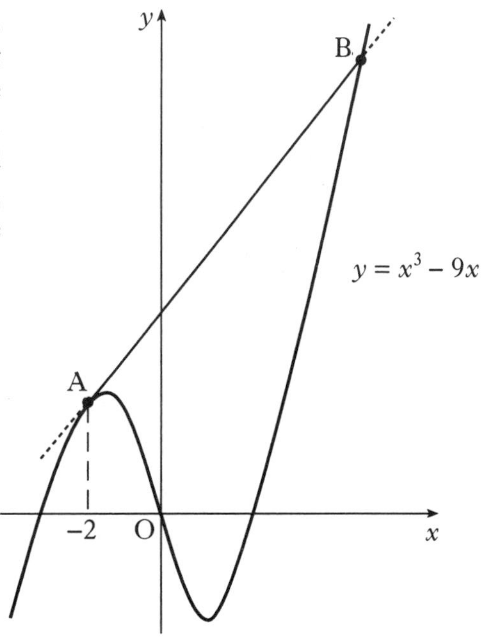

(*a*) (i) Write down the coordinates of A.

(ii) Find the equation of the line AB. **(4)**

(*b*) Determine the coordinates of the point B which represents the northern end of the causeway. **(3)**

Marks

5. The functions f and g are defined on a suitable domain by

$$f(x) = x^2 - 1 \text{ and } g(x) = x^2 + 2.$$

(*a*) Find an expression for $f(g(x))$. **(2)**

(*b*) Factorise $f(g(x))$. **(2)**

6. A and B are acute angles such that $\tan A = \frac{3}{4}$ and $\tan B = \frac{5}{12}$.

Find the exact value of

(*a*) $\sin 2A$ **(2)**

(*b*) $\cos 2A$ **(2)**

(*c*) $\sin(2A + B)$. **(2)**

7. Two sequences are defined by these recurrence relations

$$u_{n+1} = 3u_n - 0 \cdot 4 \text{ with } u_0 = 1, \qquad v_{n+1} = 0 \cdot 3v_n + 4 \text{ with } v_0 = 1.$$

(*a*) Explain why only one of these sequences approaches a limit as $n \to \infty$. **(1)**

(*b*) Find algebraically the exact value of the limit. **(2)**

8. A curve, for which $\frac{dy}{dx} = 6x^2 - 2x$, passes through the point $(-1, 2)$.

Express y in terms of x. **(3)**

Marks

9. The diagram shows a sketch of the curve $y = x^3 + kx^2 - 8x + 3$. The tangent to the curve at $x = -2$ is parallel to the x-axis.

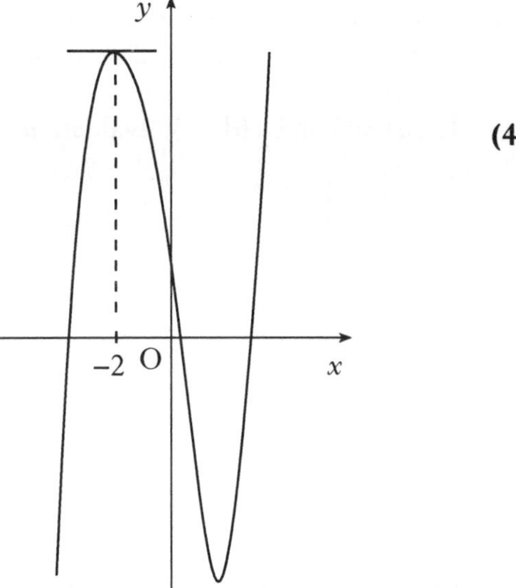

Find the value of k. **(4)**

10. A sketch of part of the graph of $y = \sin 2x$ is shown in the diagram.

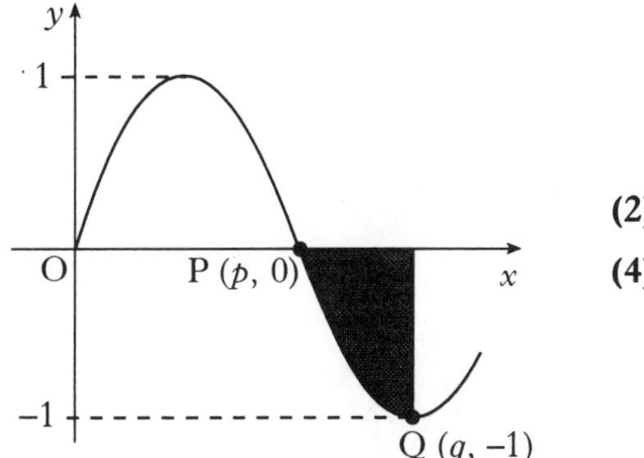

The points P and Q have coordinates $(p, 0)$ and $(q, -1)$.

(*a*) Write down the values of p and q. **(2)**

(*b*) Find the area of the shaded region. **(4)**

Marks

11. The diagram shows representatives of two vectors, $\boldsymbol{a}$ and $\boldsymbol{b}$, inclined at an angle of 60°.

If $|\boldsymbol{a}| = 2$ and $|\boldsymbol{b}| = 3$, evaluate $\boldsymbol{a}.(\boldsymbol{a} + \boldsymbol{b})$. **(3)**

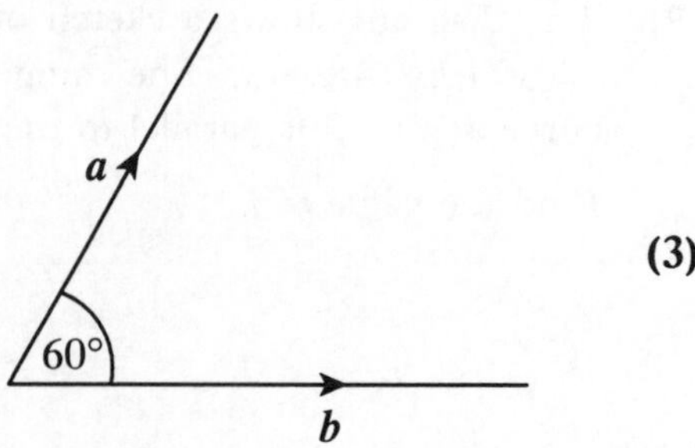

12. (*a*) Write the equation $\cos 2\theta + 8\cos\theta + 9 = 0$ in terms of $\cos\theta$ and show that, for $\cos\theta$, it has equal roots. **(3)**

(*b*) Show that there are no real roots for θ. **(2)**

[*END OF QUESTION PAPER*]

Refer to page 3 for Instructions to Candidates

All questions should be attempted

Marks

1. A triangle ABC has vertices A(2, –1, 3), B(3, 6, 5) and C(6, 6, –2).

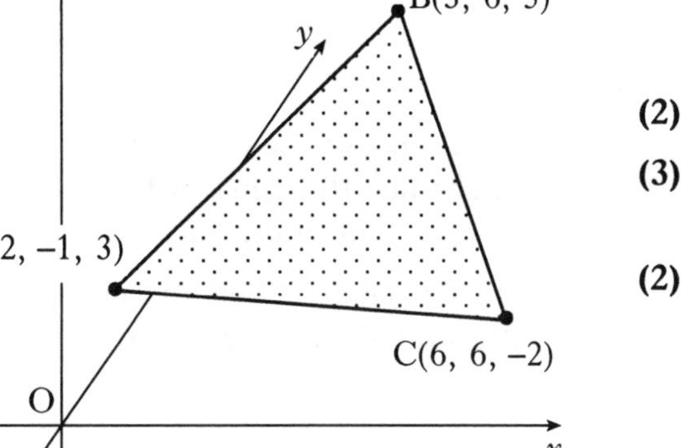

(*a*) Find $\overrightarrow{AB}$ and $\overrightarrow{AC}$. **(2)**

(*b*) Calculate the size of angle BAC. **(3)**

(*c*) Hence find the area of the triangle. **(2)**

2. A curve has equation $y = -x^4 + 4x^3 - 2$. An incomplete sketch of the graph is shown in the diagram.

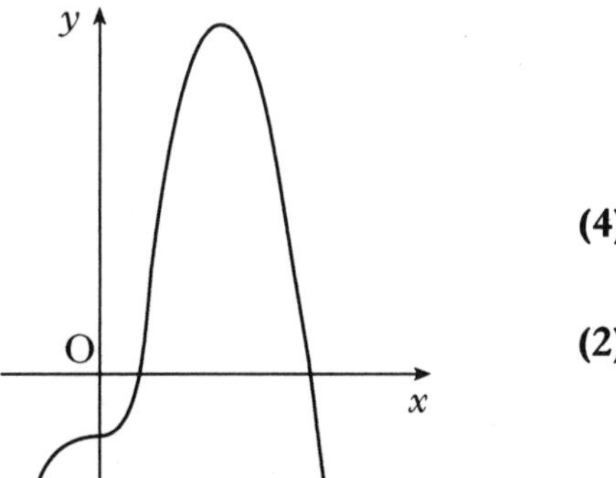

(*a*) Find the coordinates of the stationary points. **(4)**

(*b*) Determine the nature of the stationary points. **(2)**

Marks

3. (*a*) The diagram shows an incomplete sketch of the curve with equation $y = x^3 - 4x^2 + 2x - 1$.

Find the equation of the tangent to the curve at the point P where $x = 2$. **(3)**

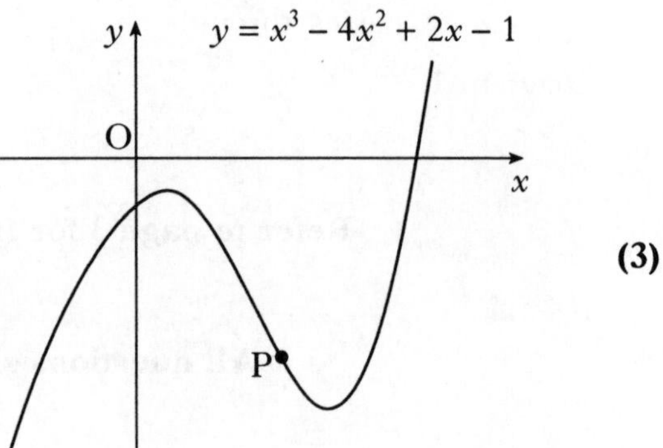

(*b*) The normal to the curve at P is defined as the straight line through P which is perpendicular to the tangent to the curve at P.

Find the angle which the normal at P makes with the positive direction of the x-axis. **(2)**

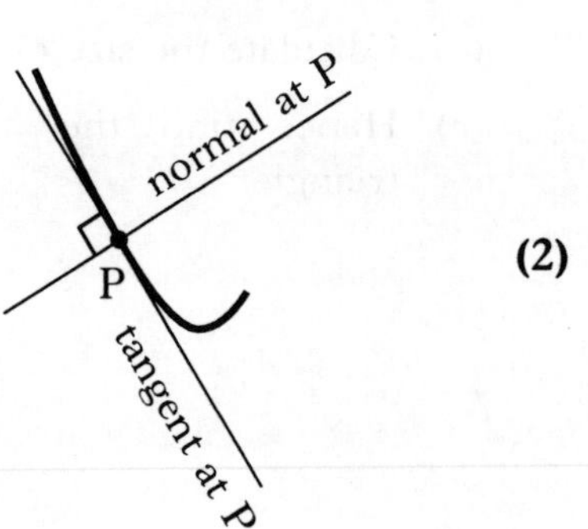

Marks

4. A parabola passes through the points (0, 0), (6, 0) and (3, 9) as shown in Diagram 1.

Diagram 1

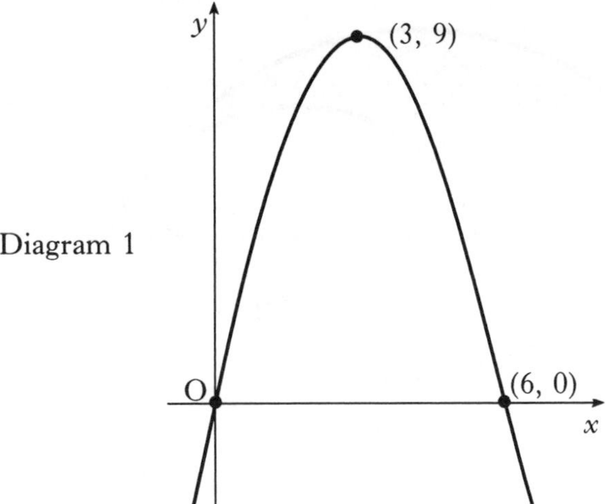

(*a*) The parabola has equation of the form $y = ax(b - x)$.

Determine the values of a and b. **(2)**

(*b*) Find the area enclosed by the parabola and the x-axis. **(3)**

Diagram 2

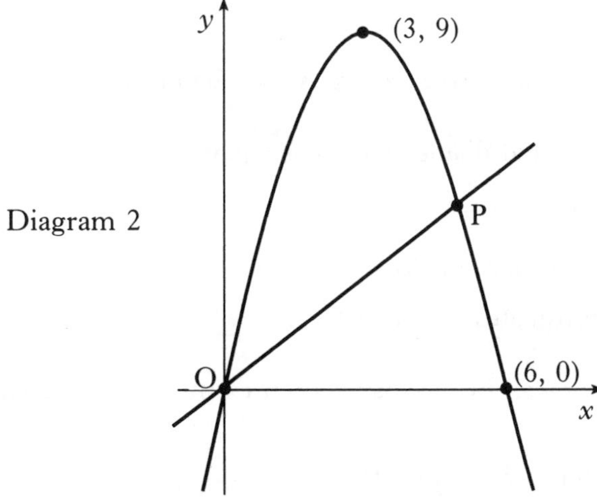

(*c*) (i) Diagram 2 shows the parabola from (*a*) and the straight line with equation $y = x$. Find the coordinates of P, the point of intersection of the parabola and the line.

(ii) Calculate the area enclosed between the parabola and the line. **(5)**

Marks

5. The perimeter of the shape shown in the diagram is composed of 3 semicircles with centres A, B and C which lie on a straight line.

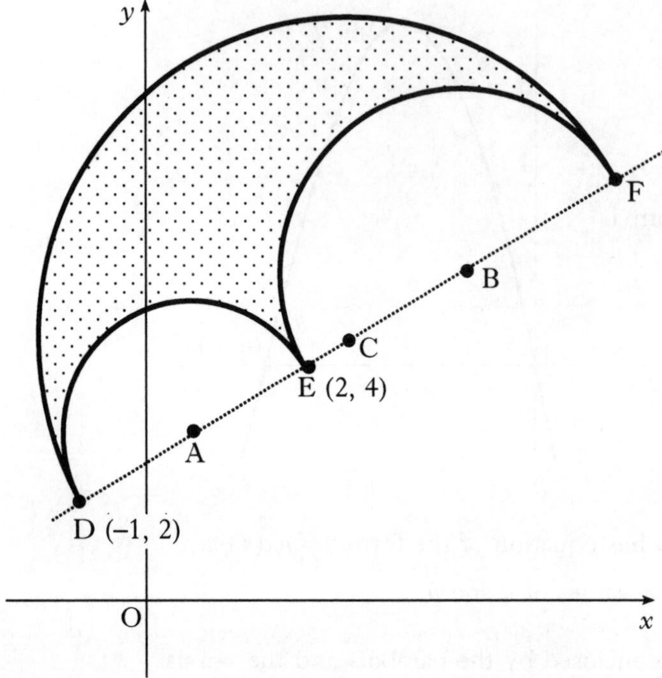

DE is a diameter of one of the semicircles. The coordinates of D and E are (−1, 2) and (2, 4).

(*a*) Find the equation of the circle with centre A and diameter DE. **(2)**

The circle with centre B and diameter EF has equation

$$x^2 + y^2 - 16x - 16y + 76 = 0.$$

(*b*) (i) Write down the coordinates of B.

(ii) Determine the coordinates of F and C. **(3)**

(*c*) In the diagram the perimeter of the shape is represented by the thick black line.

Show that the perimeter is $5\pi\sqrt{13}$ units. **(3)**

Marks

6. The function f is defined by $f(x) = 2\cos x° - 3\sin x°$.

(*a*) Show that $f(x)$ can be expressed in the form $f(x) = k\cos(x + \alpha)°$ where $k > 0$ and $0 \leq \alpha < 360$, and determine the values of k and α. **(3)**

(*b*) Hence find the maximum and minimum values of $f(x)$ and the values of x at which they occur, where x lies in the interval $0 \leq x < 360$. **(3)**

(*c*) Write down the minimum value of $(f(x))^2$. **(1)**

7. A gardener feeds her trees weekly with "Bioforce, the wonder plant food". It is known that in a week the amount of plant food in the tree falls by about 25% .

(*a*) The trees contain no Bioforce initially and the gardener applies 1 g of Bioforce to each tree every Saturday. Bioforce is only effective when there is continuously more than 2 g of it in the tree. Calculate how many weekly feeds will be necessary before the Bioforce becomes effective. **(2)**

(*b*) (i) Write down a recurrence relation for the amount of plant food in the tree immediately after feeding.

(ii) If the level of Bioforce in the tree exceeds 5 g, it will cause leaf burn. Is it safe to continue feeding the trees at this rate indefinitely? **(3)**

Marks

8. A child's drinking beaker is in the shape of a cylinder with a hemispherical lid and a circular flat base. The radius of the cylinder is r cm and the height is h cm. The volume of the cylinder is $400\,\text{cm}^3$.

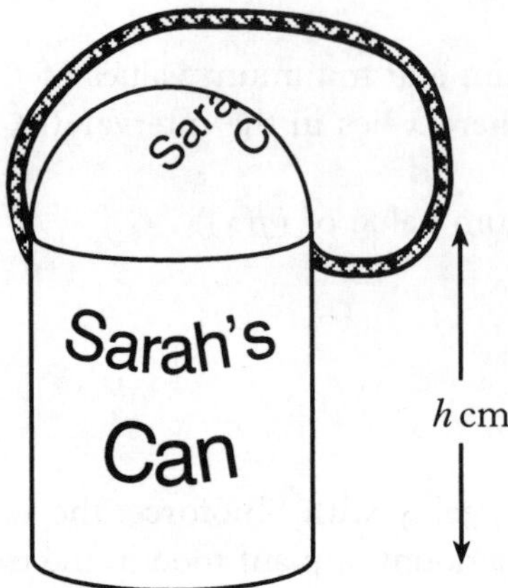

(*a*) Show that the surface area of plastic, $A(r)$, needed to make the beaker is given by $A(r) = 3\pi r^2 + \dfrac{800}{r}$. **(2)**

Note: The curved surface area of a hemisphere of radius r is $2\pi r^2$.

(*b*) Find the value of r which ensures that the surface area of plastic is minimised. **(4)**

9. (*a*) The variables x and y are connected by a relationship of the form $y = ae^{bx}$ where a and b are constants. Show that there is a linear relationship between $\log_e y$ and x. **(2)**

(*b*) From an experiment some data was obtained. The table shows the data which lies on the line of best fit.

x	3·1	3·5	4·1	5·2
y	21 876	72 631	439 392	11 913 076

The variables x and y in the above table are connected by a relationship of the form $y = ae^{bx}$. Determine the values of a and b. **(4)**

[*END OF QUESTION PAPER*]

NATIONAL QUALIFICATIONS

MODEL PAPER G

MATHEMATICS
HIGHER
Paper 1
(Non-calculator)

Refer to page 3 for Instructions to Candidates

All questions should be attempted

Marks

1. (*a*) Show that $x = 2$ is a root of the equation $2x^3 + x^2 - 13x + 6 = 0$. **(1)**

(*b*) Hence find the other roots. **(3)**

2. A and B are the points (–3, –1) and (5, 5).

Find the equation of

(*a*) the line AB **(2)**

(*b*) the perpendicular bisector of AB. **(3)**

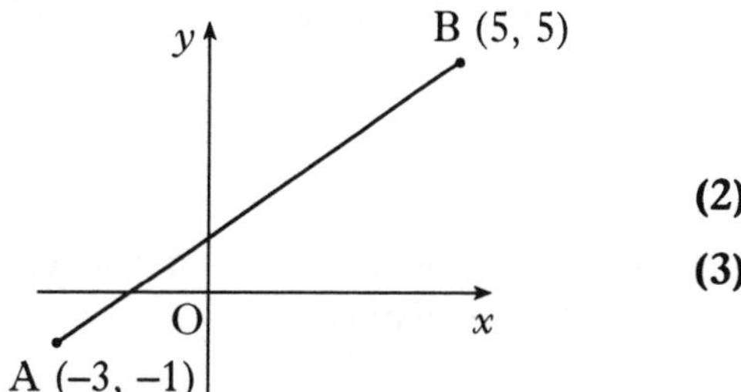

3. The line PQ has equation $y = 2x + 4$.

(*a*) Find, without using calculus, the area of the shaded trapezium shown in the diagram. **(2)**

(*b*) Express the area of this trapezium as a definite integral. **(1)**

(*c*) Evaluate this integral. **(2)**

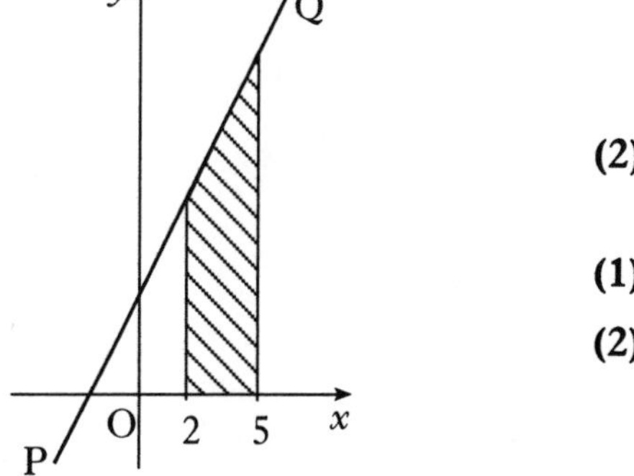

Marks

4. (*a*) The diagram shows a circle, centre P, with equation $x^2 + y^2 + 6x + 4y + 8 = 0$.

Find the equation of the tangent at the point A (–1, –1) on the circle. **(3)**

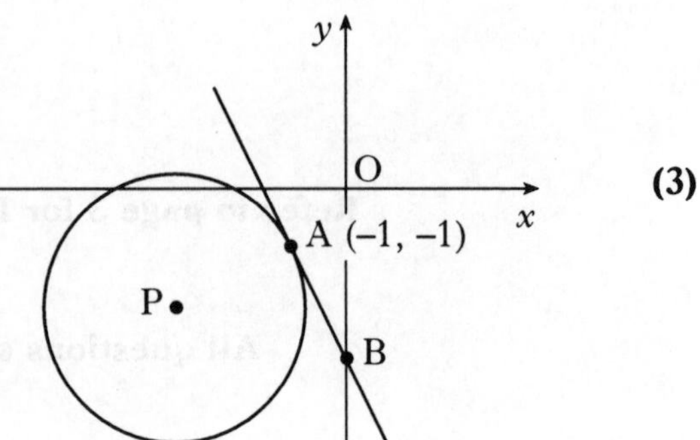

(*b*) The tangent crosses the y-axis at B.

Find the coordinates of B. **(1)**

(*c*) Another circle, centre P, is drawn passing through B. The tangent at A meets the second circle at the point C, as shown in the diagram.

Write down the coordinates of C. **(1)**

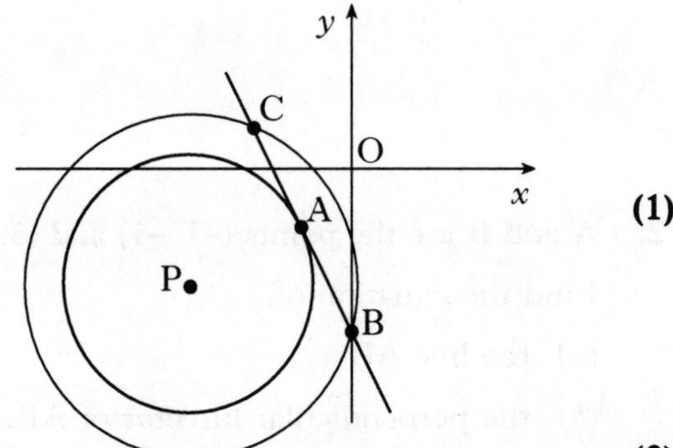

(*d*) Find the equation of the circle with BC as diameter. **(2)**

Marks

5. VABCD is a pyramid with rectangular base ABCD.

The vectors $\overrightarrow{AB}$, $\overrightarrow{AD}$ and $\overrightarrow{AV}$ are given by

$\overrightarrow{AB} = 8\boldsymbol{i} + 2\boldsymbol{j} + 2\boldsymbol{k}$

$\overrightarrow{AD} = -2\boldsymbol{i} + 10\boldsymbol{j} - 2\boldsymbol{k}$ and

$\overrightarrow{AV} = \boldsymbol{i} + 7\boldsymbol{j} + 7\boldsymbol{k}$.

Express $\overrightarrow{CV}$ in component form. **(3)**

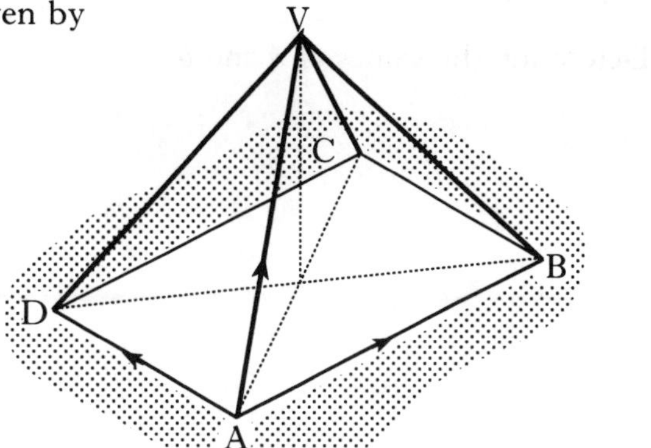

6. Part of the graph of $y = f(x)$ is shown in the diagram. On separate diagrams, sketch the graph of

(*a*) $y = f(x + 1)$ **(4)**

(*b*) $y = -2f(x)$. **(2)**

Indicate on each graph the images of O, A, B, C and D.

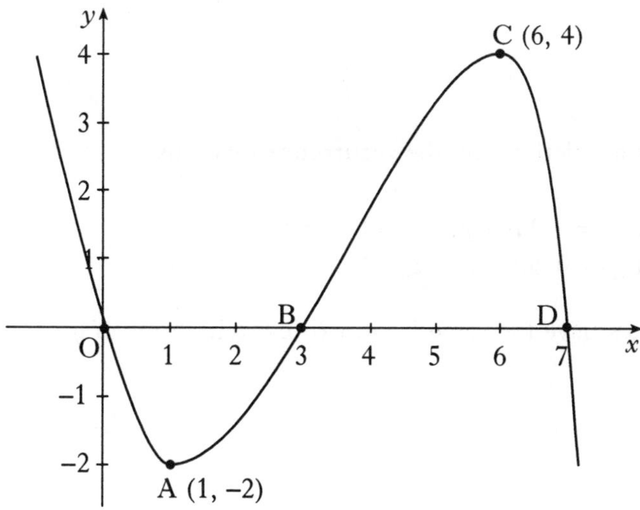

Marks

7. The diagram shows part of the graph of

$y = \log_b(x + a)$.

Determine the values of a and b. **(3)**

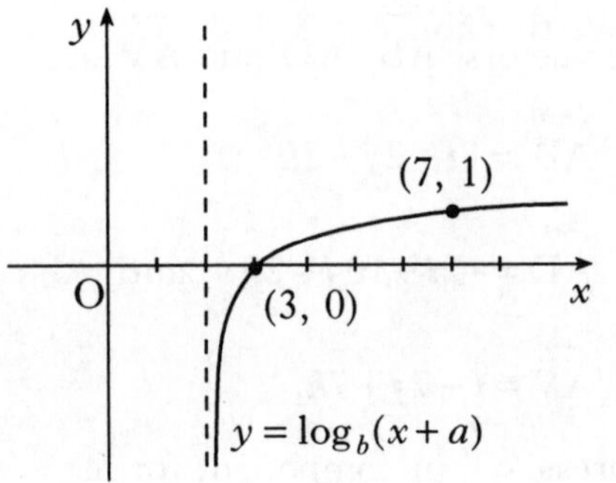

8. The diagram shows two vectors $\boldsymbol{a}$ and $\boldsymbol{b}$, with $|\boldsymbol{a}| = 3$ and $|\boldsymbol{b}| = 2\sqrt{2}$.

These vectors are inclined at an angle of 45° to each other.

(*a*) Evaluate (i) $\boldsymbol{a.a}$

(ii) $\boldsymbol{b.b}$

(iii) $\boldsymbol{a.b}$ **(2)**

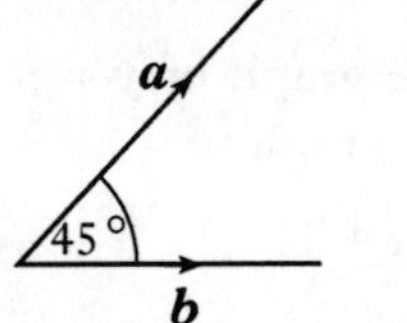

(*b*) Another vector $\boldsymbol{p}$ is defined by $\boldsymbol{p} = 2\boldsymbol{a} + 3\boldsymbol{b}$.

Evaluate $\boldsymbol{p.p}$ and hence write down $|\boldsymbol{p}|$. **(4)**

9 Two sequences are defined by the recurrence relations

$$u_{n+1} = 0\cdot 2u_n + p, \quad u_0 = 1 \quad \text{and}$$
$$v_{n+1} = 0\cdot 6v_n + q, \quad v_0 = 1.$$

If both sequences have the same limit, express p in terms of q. **(4)**

Marks

10. A curve has equation $y = 2x^3 + 3x^2 + 4x - 5$.

Prove that this curve has no stationary points. **(5)**

11. Given $f(x) = \cos^2 x - \sin^2 x$, find $f'(x)$. **(4)**

[END OF QUESTION PAPER]

NATIONAL QUALIFICATIONS

MODEL PAPER G

MATHEMATICS HIGHER Paper 2

Refer to page 3 for Instructions to Candidates

All questions should be attempted

Marks

1. A triangle ABC has vertices A (−4, 1), B (12, 3) and C (7, −7).

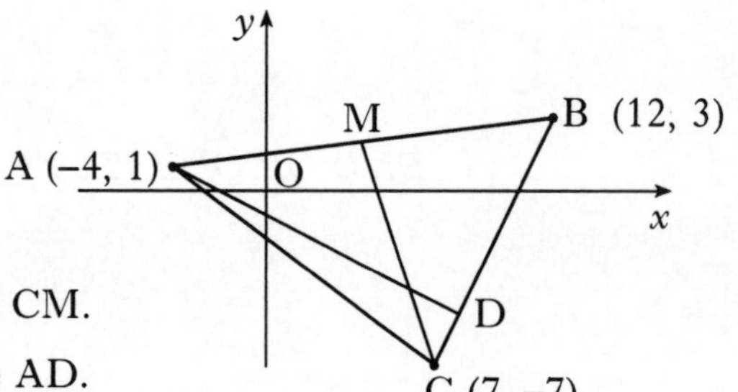

(*a*) Find the equation of the median CM. **(3)**

(*b*) Find the equation of the altitude AD. **(3)**

(*c*) Find the coordinates of the point of intersection of CM and AD. **(2)**

2. The point P(−1, 7) lies on the curve with equation $y = 5x^2 + 2$. Find the equation of the tangent to the curve at P. **(4)**

Marks

3. ABCDEFGH is a cuboid.

K lies two thirds of the way along HG, (ie HK:KG = 2:1).

L lies one quarter of the way along FG, (ie FL:LG = 1:3).

$\overrightarrow{AB}$, $\overrightarrow{AD}$ and $\overrightarrow{AE}$ can be represented by the vectors

$\begin{pmatrix} 3 \\ 6 \\ 3 \end{pmatrix}$, $\begin{pmatrix} -8 \\ 4 \\ 4 \end{pmatrix}$ and $\begin{pmatrix} 1 \\ -3 \\ 5 \end{pmatrix}$ respectively.

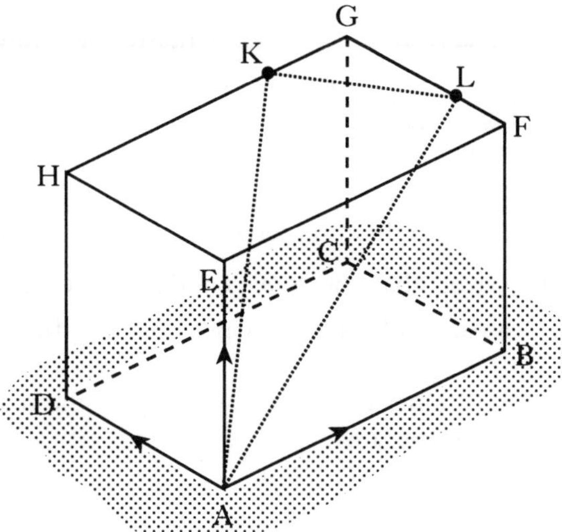

(*a*) Calculate the components of $\overrightarrow{AK}$. **(2)**

(*b*) Calculate the components of $\overrightarrow{AL}$. **(2)**

(*c*) Calculate the size of angle KAL. **(4)**

4. The parabola shown in the diagram has equation $y = 4x - x^2$ and intersects the x-axis at the origin and P.

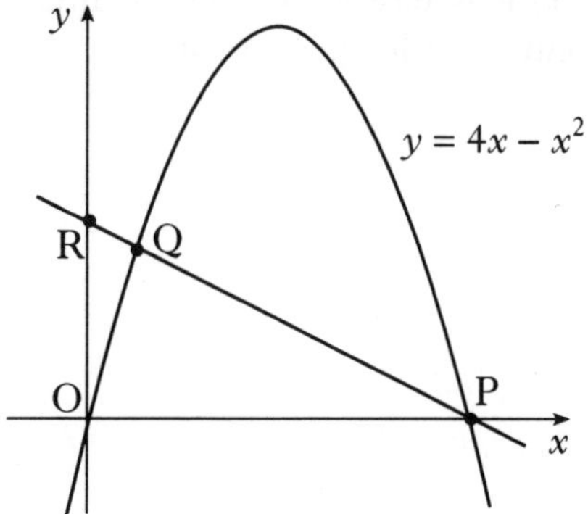

(*a*) Find the coordinates of the point P. **(2)**

(*b*) R is the point (0, 2). Find the equation of PR. **(2)**

(*c*) The line and the parabola also intersect at Q. Find the coordinates of Q. **(3)**

Marks

5. A zookeeper wants to fence off six individual animal pens.

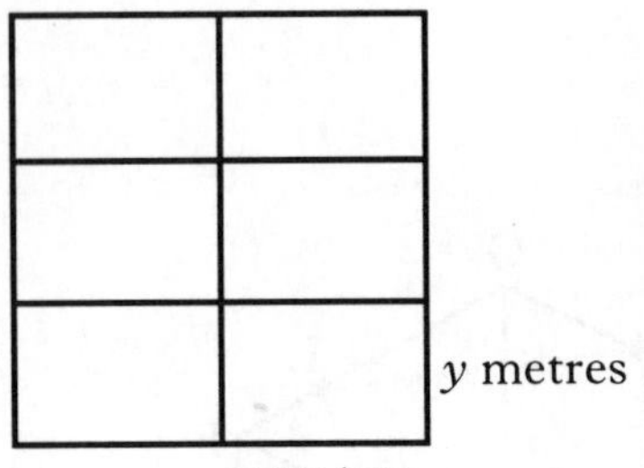

Each pen is a rectangle measuring x metres by y metres, as shown in the diagram.

(*a*) (i) Express the total length of fencing in terms of x and y.

(ii) Given that the total length of fencing is 360 m, show that the total area, $A\,\text{m}^2$, of the six pens is given by $A(x) = 240x - \frac{16}{3}x^2$. **(3)**

(*b*) Find the values of x and y which give the maximum area and write down this maximum area. **(5)**

6. The intensity I_t of light is reduced as it passes through a filter according to the law $I_t = I_0 e^{-kt}$ where I_0 is the initial intensity and I_t is the intensity after passing through a filter of thickness t cm. k is a constant.

(*a*) A filter of thickness 4 cm reduces the intensity from 120 candle-power to 90 candle-power. Find the value of k. **(3)**

(*b*) Light is passed through a filter of thickness 10 cm. Find the percentage reduction in its intensity. **(3)**

Marks

7. The diagram shows a circle of radius 1 unit and centre the origin. The radius OP makes an angle $a°$ with the positive direction of the x-axis.

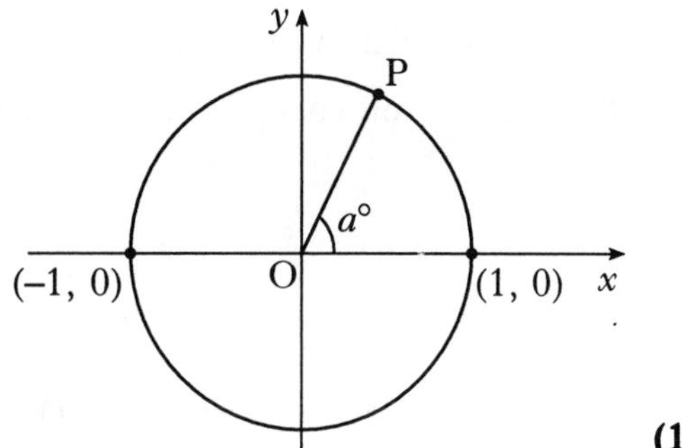

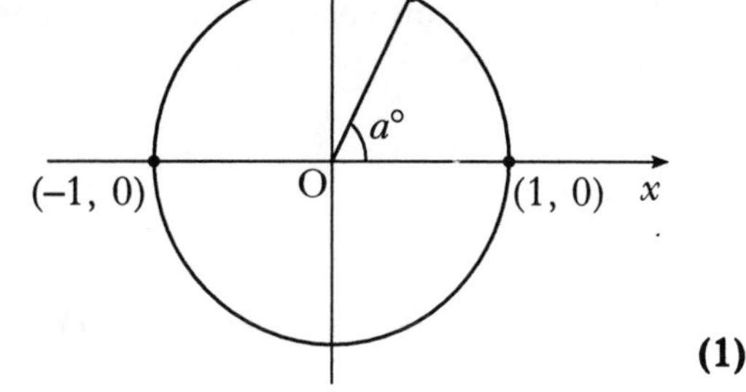

(*a*) Show that P is the point $(\cos a°, \sin a°)$. **(1)**

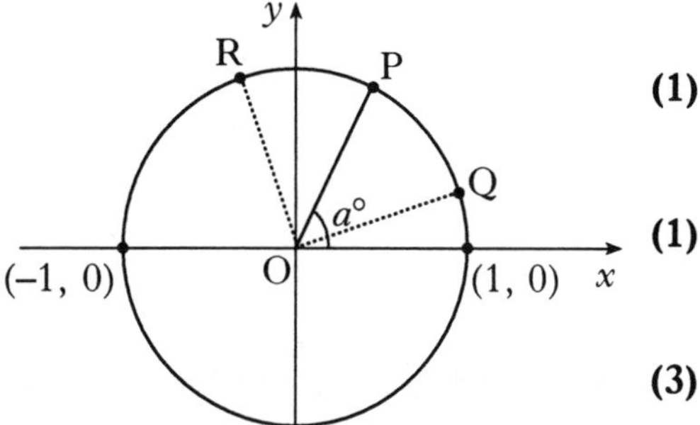

(*b*) If $P\hat{O}Q = 45°$, deduce the coordinates of Q in terms of a. **(1)**

(*c*) If $P\hat{O}R = 45°$, deduce the coordinates of R in terms of a. **(1)**

(*d*) Hence find an expression for the gradient of QR in its simplest form. **(3)**

8. Solve the equation $2\sin x° - 3\cos x° = 2 \cdot 5$ in the interval $0 \leq x < 360$. **(6)**

Marks

9. The origin, O, and the points P and Q are the vertices of a curved "triangle" which is shaded in the diagram.

The sides lie on curves with equations $y = x(x+3)$, $y = x - \frac{1}{4}x^2$ and $y = \frac{4}{x^2}$.

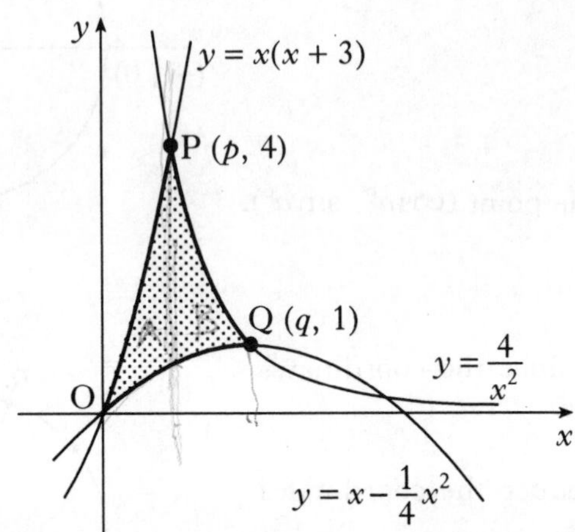

(*a*) P and Q have coordinates (p, 4) and (q, 1). Find the values of p and q. **(2)**

(*b*) Calculate the shaded area. **(5)**

[*END OF QUESTION PAPER*]

MODEL PAPER A — HIGHER MATHEMATICS ANSWERS

PAPER I

1. *(a)* $\begin{pmatrix} 2 \\ 1 \\ -2 \end{pmatrix}$ *(b)* 3 units

2. *(a)* $3y = 2x + 13$ *(b)* Proof {$(-5, 1)$ satisfies equation (a)}

3. $f(x) = x^2 - 3x + 4$ **4.** *(a)* $x + 2y = 2$ *(b)* $(x-4)^2 + (y+1)^2 = 45$

5. Proof

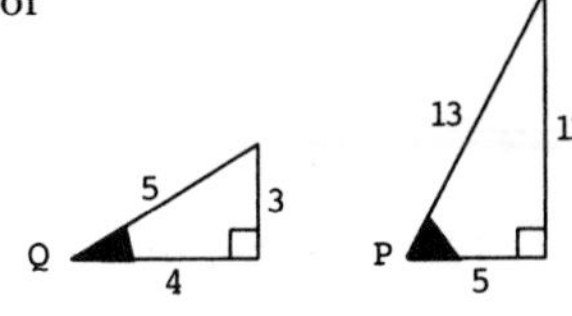

6. $p = -17$ and $x = 2$ or $\frac{5}{2}$ are the other roots

7.

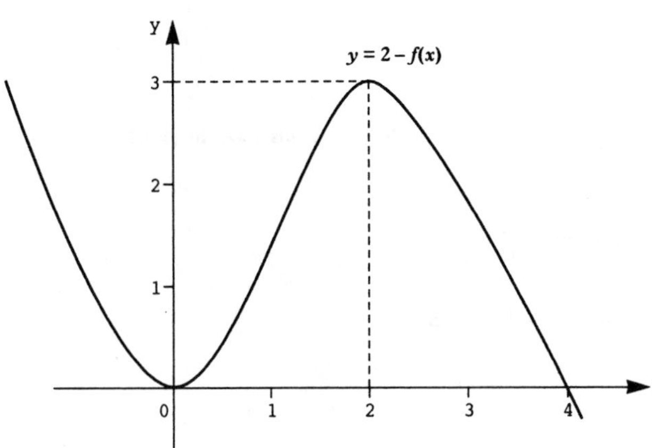

8. $\frac{2}{\sqrt{x}} - 6\sin 2x$

9. *(a)* Proof *(b)* $x - \frac{1}{2}\cos 2x + c$

10. $\frac{2}{9}(1 + 3x)^{3/2} + c$; $\frac{14}{9}$

11. $q = p^2$; $q = 25$

PAPER II

1. Minimum T.P. at $\left(-\frac{1}{2}, -\frac{27}{16}\right)$. Point of Inflexion at (1,0)

2. *(a)* A(−12, 0); B(12, 0) *(b)* £816

3. *(a)* $k(x) = 5 - 4x$ *(b)* $h(k(x)) = x$ *(c)* $h = k^{-1}(x)$ { ***inverses*** }

4. *(a)* B(−2, 5) *(b)* $m_{\text{road}} = m_{\text{circuit}}$ at B or double route implies tangency

5. *(a)* 13·05 *(b)* 3 doses *(c)* Proof $\{u_{n+1} = 0\cdot85^{+}u_n + 25\}$
(d) No, as limit 52·3 < 55

6. *(a)* Proof {various methods e.g. Cosine Rule}
(b) $8\sqrt{5}\sin(\theta - 63\cdot4)°$ *(c)* $\theta = 114\cdot9$

7. *(a)* $\log_e I = -\frac{4}{5}\log_e t + 4$ *(b)* Proof; $k = 54\cdot6$, $r = -\frac{4}{5}$

8. *(a)* Proof {use Pythagoras}
(b) Proof {use differentiation}; £127 million, 109 km

MODEL PAPER B — HIGHER MATHEMATICS ANSWERS

PAPER I

1. $\frac{3}{4}x^4 + 2x^2 + c$

2. Proof {show that $\vec{RS} = 3\vec{ST}$}

3. *(a)* Proof; $f(x-1) = 4x^2 - 11x + 12$; Proof *(b)* $4x + 7$ *(c)* $6x + 5$ {$h'(x)$}

4. $\underline{u} + \underline{v} = \begin{pmatrix} -2 \\ 8 \\ 2 \end{pmatrix}$; $\underline{u} - \underline{v} = \begin{pmatrix} -4 \\ -2 \\ 4 \end{pmatrix}$; Proof {use scalar product}

5. *(a)* A(6, 6); B(−2, −2)
   (b) $(x-2)^2 + (y-2)^2 = 32$ OR $x^2 + y^2 - 4x - 4y - 24 = 0$

6. *(a)* $u_2 = 4\cdot 7$ *(b)* $n = 3$ *(c)* Limit $= 20$

7. $f(x) = (x+4)^2 + 2$; min T.P. at (−4, 2)

8. *(a)* $\frac{24}{25}$ *(b)* $\frac{336}{625}$

9. $m = \sqrt{3}$; angle = 15°

10.  *(a)*

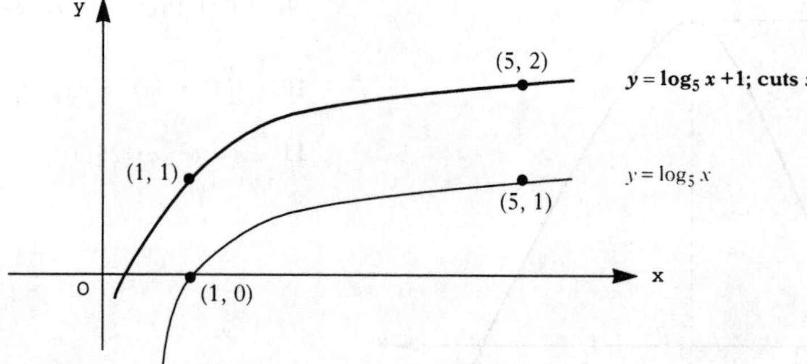

(b)

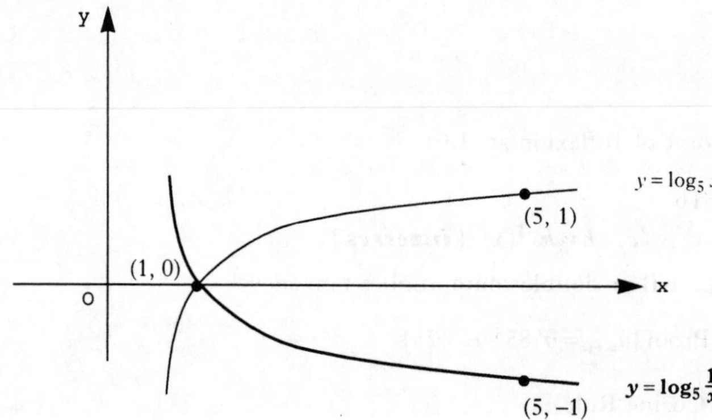

11. $3\sin^2 x \cos x$; $\frac{1}{3}\sin^3 x + c$

PAPER II

1. *(a)* $a = 6$; point $(0, 6)$ *(b)* $(-3, 0)$ and $\left(\frac{1}{2}, 0\right)$

2. *(a)* $2x + y = 10$ *(b)* D(4, 2) *(c)* Area = 5 units^2

3. *(a)* B(6, 4, 2); C(4, 3, 4); D(6, 2, 2) *(b)* Mid-point of AD = (4, 3, 4) = C

   (c) $\angle AOB = 44 \cdot 4^\circ$ *(d)* $\angle OAB = 67 \cdot 8^\circ$

4. *(a)* (i) Distance $\doteqdot 78 \cdot 3$ $\{5\sqrt{245}\}$ (ii) Clearance $\doteqdot 13 \cdot 3$ cm

   (b) (i) $m_{PB} = 1$ (ii) $x + y = 10$; A(8, 2) and C(6, 4)

5. *(a)* $\sqrt{10}\,\sin(x - 18 \cdot 4)^\circ$ *(b)* $x = 63 \cdot 4,\ 153 \cdot 4$

6. *(a)* 409·37 g *(b)* 34·7 years *(c)*

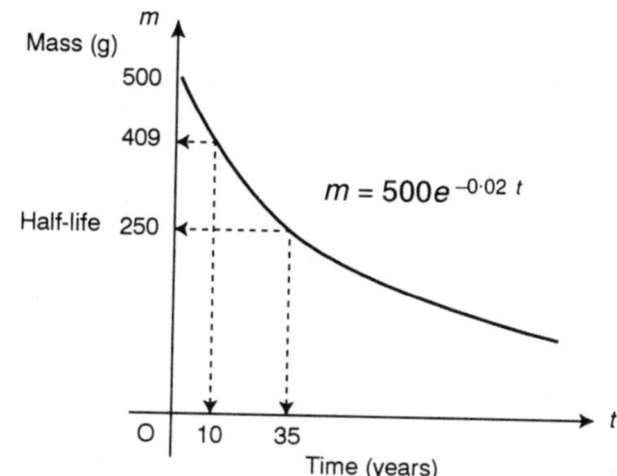

7. *(a)* Proof {area of rectangle – area of 3 Δs} *(b)* Greatest area = 24 units^2; Least area = 16 units^2

8. *(a)* $p = \frac{-1}{2}(q+2)$ *(b)* $p = -3$; $y = x^2 - 3x + 4$

   (c) Discriminant = −7 {No real roots}. The curve does not cross the x-axis

9. Area $= \frac{208}{3}$ m^2; Volume = 4160 m^3

MODEL PAPER C — HIGHER MATHEMATICS ANSWERS

PAPER I

1. *(a)* Proof *(b)* $f(x) = (x+4)(2x+1)(x-3)$

2. $2x^3 - \frac{x^2}{2} + \sin x + C$

3. *(a)* Proof {Hint: show AB = AC } *(b)* (i) $H\left(4, \frac{7}{2}\right)$ (ii) Proof

4. $-\frac{8}{x^3} + \frac{3}{2}\sqrt{x}$

5. *(a)* $\frac{x^2-2}{x^2-4}$ *(b)* $x \neq \pm 2$

6. $\frac{3\sqrt{11}}{10}$

7. $-\frac{1}{3}$

8. $y = 10x^2$

9. $a = 3$; $b = 2$

10. $k = +5$ or -3

11. *(a)* 20 m s^{-1}
(b) 0, Ball is stationary at a point where $h = 20$. This is its maximum height.

12. $k = \sqrt{8}$, $x = 45$

PAPER II

1. YES; Belligerent will

2. *(a)* Proof {Hint: use $y - f(2) = f'(2)(x-2)$} *(b)* $(-2, -18)$

3. Pestkill

4. *(a)* (i) $a = 3$; $b = 2$ (ii) $d = 3$; $c = 3$
(b) $h(x) = \sqrt{13}\sin(3x + 56\cdot3)^\circ$; $p = 3$; $q = \sqrt{13}$; $r = 56\cdot3$

5. *(a)* $|\vec{BR}| = 2\sqrt{69}$ km (approx. 16·6 km) *(b)* 429 km/hr
(c) Proof ($\vec{BR}.\vec{TC} = 0$) *(d)* $36\cdot7^\circ$

6. $a = -\frac{1}{3}$; $b = \frac{1}{3}$; $c = 3$

7. $(x-4)^2 + (y+3)^2 = 225$

8. *(a)* 48 units^2 *(b)* Proof$\left\{\text{Hint: use } \int_0^p \left(2x - \frac{x^2}{6}\right) dx = 24\right\}$
(c) (i) Proof (ii) $p \doteqdot -4\cdot4$ or $16\cdot4$ (iii) $-4\cdot4 < 0$ and $16\cdot4 > 12$

9. *(a)* Proof *(b)* Proof$\left\{\text{Hint: solve } \frac{dT}{dx} = 0\right\}$ *(c)* $x = 4$; $T = 10$

MODEL PAPER D — HIGHER MATHEMATICS ANSWERS

PAPER I

1. $2x + y = 10$ **2.** Ratio 2 : 3 **3.** $x(x-1)(x^2+x+1)$

4. (i) (ii)

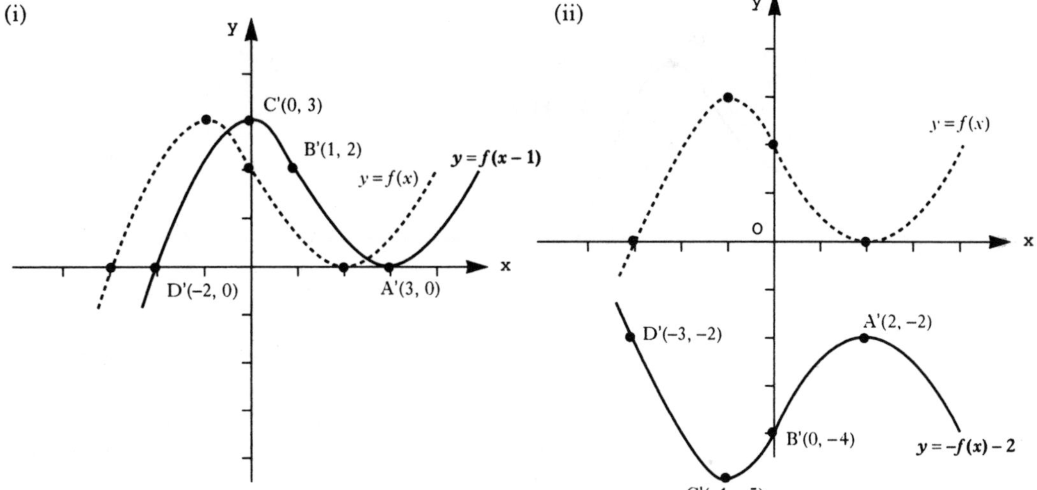

5. $\frac{5}{16}$ **6.** *(a)* This sequence has a limit since $0{\cdot}3 < 1$ {i.e. the coefficient of U_n) *(b)* $\frac{50}{7}$

7. *(a)* (i) $g(f(x)) = 4x^2 + 4x + 1 + k$ (ii) $f(g(x)) = 2x^2 + 2k + 1$

(b) (i) Proof (ii) When $k = 6$ the roots are real, distinct and rational

(iii) $k = -2$ for equal roots

8. Proof {Hint: use $\cos(x+y) = \cos x^\circ \cos y^\circ - \sin x^\circ \sin y^\circ$} **9.** $x < -2$ and $x > 3$

10. $\sin x^\circ = \frac{4\sqrt{5}}{9}$ **11.** *(a)* $k = 0{\cdot}1$ *(b)* 9 °C

12. $(x-3)^2 + (y-4)^2 = 25$ or $x^2 + y^2 - 6x - 8y = 0$

PAPER II

1. *(a)* (0, 3) and (3, −24) *(b)* Point of inflection (0,3); Min T.P. (3, −24)

2. *(a)* Proof {Hint: show $m_{AB} \times m_{BC} = -1$}

(b) (i) Eqn_{AD} $3y = x - 6$; Eqn_{BE} $3y = -4x - 1$ (ii) Hence $M\left(1, \frac{-5}{3}\right)$

3. *(a)* Q(2, 2, 9); R(21, 3, 12) *(b)* $Q\hat{P}R = 83{\cdot}4^\circ$

4. Area $= 1 - \frac{\sqrt{3}}{4}$ units² $\{\doteqdot 0{\cdot}567\}$

5. *(a)* Limit 6·25 is endangered *(b)* Limit 4·375 is safe; grant permission

6. *(a)* $x = 0, 70{\cdot}5, 180, 289{\cdot}5, 360$ *(b)* $f(x) = 2\sin x^\circ$; $g(x) = 3\sin 2x^\circ$

(c) A(70·5, 1·89); B(289·5, −1·89) *(d)* $70{\cdot}5 < x < 180$; $289{\cdot}5 < x < 360$

7. *(a)* $y = \frac{4}{3}x - 50$ *(b)* $x^2 + y^2 = 900$ *(c)* Proof; P = (24, −18)

8. *(a)* $\frac{4}{3}$ unit² *(b)* $p \doteqdot 2{\cdot}3$ *(c)* Proof; $q = 2{\cdot}3$ approx

MODEL PAPER E — HIGHER MATHEMATICS ANSWERS

PAPER I

1. (a) Eqn CE is $y = -3x + 5$; Eqn BD is $y = x + 1$ (b) J(1, 2)

2. (a) (b)

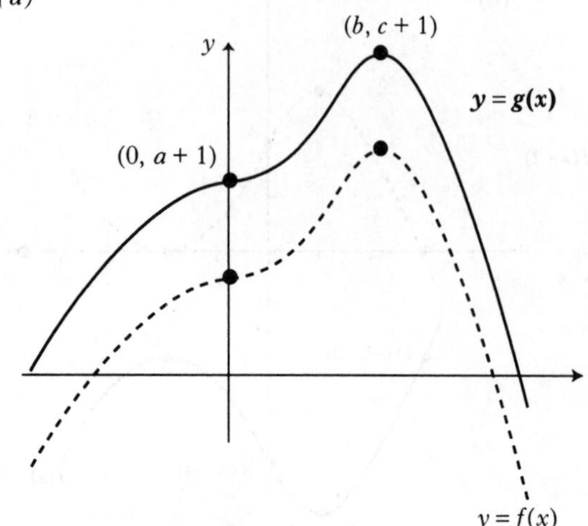

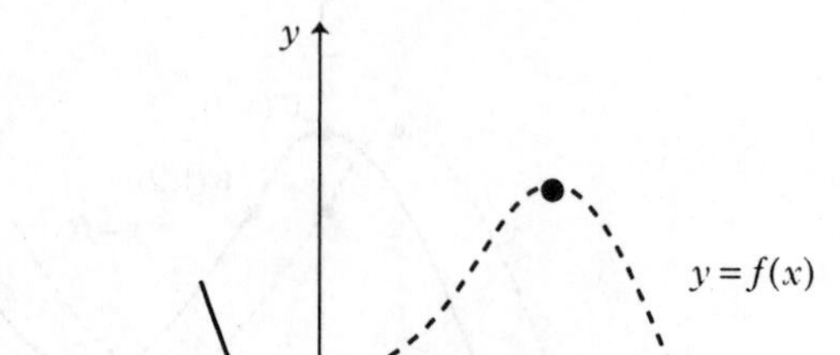

(c) They are the SAME

3. A(−4·5, 0); B(45, 0)

4. $x = -1$

5. (a) Proof (b) Proof $\left\{\text{use } \tan a° = \dfrac{\sin a°}{\cos a°}\right\}$

6. $\dfrac{dy}{dx} = 4x + 1$; Proof {Hint; show LHS = RHS

7. $f(x) = \dfrac{1}{2}\sin 2x + \dfrac{3}{4}$

8. $(x-13)^2 + (y-4)^2 = 17$

9. $\underline{a} \cdot (\underline{b} + \underline{c}) = 0$; $\underline{a}$ is perpendicular to $(\underline{b} + \underline{c})$

10. $a = 45°$

11. (a) $\dfrac{-1}{a^2}$ (b) Proof $\left\{\text{Hint: use } A\left(a, \dfrac{1}{a}\right) \text{ and } m = \dfrac{-1}{a^2}\right\}$

(c) (i) 2 units² (ii) Area is independent of A's position.

12. $k = 5$

PAPER II

1. (a) $k = 3$ (b) $(x-2)(x+2)(x+3)$
2. (a) A(1, 3); B(−3, −5) (b) (i) C(−5, 1) (ii) $x + 2y + 3 = 0$
3. (a) R(7, −1, 6) (b) ∠PSR = 84·6°
4. (a) £1537.93 (b) November 1st (c) $A_{n+1} = 1\cdot005A_n + 100$ {Original amount A_0 = £1000}
5. (a) $\sin x° - 3\cos x° = \sqrt{10}\sin(x - 71\cdot6)°$; $k = \sqrt{10}$, $\alpha = 71\cdot6$ (b) Max value = $5 + \sqrt{10}$ where $x = 161\cdot6$
6. (a) A(0, 5); B(2, 1) (b) $\dfrac{64}{3}$ units² (c) $m = 10$; $n = -1$
7. (a) $k = -0\cdot000122$ (approx) (b) 88·5%
8. (a) $p = 3$; $q = 1$; $r = -140$; $u = 230$ (b) $s = -0\cdot928$; $t = 120\cdot5$
9. (a) 0 (b) Graph of $y = \cos 2x$ — positive/negative cancel.
10. (a) (i) Proof {Hint: use similarΔs.} (ii) Proof {Hint: use Vol = $(2x)^2 \times h$}

(b) Vol = $\dfrac{16}{3}$ cm × $\dfrac{16}{3}$ cm × $\dfrac{10}{3}$ cm.

MODEL PAPER F — HIGHER MATHEMATICS ANSWERS

PAPER I

1. $y = 2x - 5$ 2. $(x+2)(x-1)(x-5)$ 3. $3x + 4y = 26$

4. *(a)* (i) A(−2, 10) (ii) $y = 3x + 16$ *(b)* B(4, 28)

5. *(a)* $(x^2+2)^2 - 1$ *(b)* $(x^2+1)(x^2+3)$ 6. *(a)* $\frac{24}{25}$ *(b)* $\frac{7}{25}$ *(c)* $\frac{323}{325}$

7. *(a)* $v_{n+1} = 0{\cdot}3\, v_n + 4$ approaches a limit since $-1 < 0{\cdot}3 < 1$ *(b)* $5\frac{5}{7}$

8. $y = 2x^3 - x^2 + 5$ 9. $k = 1$

10. *(a)* $p = \frac{\pi}{2}$; $q = \frac{3\pi}{4}$ *(b)* $\frac{1}{2}$ unit^2

11. 7

12. *(a)* $\cos^2\theta + 4\cos\theta + 4 = 0$; Proof $\{\text{Hint: show } b^2 - 4ac = 0\}$ *(b)* Proof $\{\text{Hint: show } \cos\theta < -1\}$

PAPER II

1. *(a)* $\vec{AB} = \begin{pmatrix}1\\7\\2\end{pmatrix}$; $\vec{AC} = \begin{pmatrix}4\\7\\-5\end{pmatrix}$

   (b) 51·9° *(c)* 27·4 units^2

2. *(a)* (0, −2);(3, 25)

   (b) Point of inflexion at (0, −2). Maximum turning point at (3, 25)

3. *(a)* $y = -2x - 1$ *(b)* 26·6°

4. *(a)* $a = 1$; $b = 6$ *(b)* 36 units^2

   (c) (i) P(5, 5) (ii) 20·83 units^2

5. *(a)* $\left(x-\frac{1}{2}\right)^2+(y-3)^2=\frac{13}{4}$

(b) (i) B(8, 8) (ii) F(14, 12); C$\left(\frac{13}{2}, 7\right)$

(c) Proof {Hint: add the perimeters of 3 semi-circles}

6. *(a)* $k=\sqrt{13}$; $\alpha=56\cdot3^\circ$

(b) Maximum value = $\sqrt{13}$ at $x=303\cdot7^\circ$; Minimum value = $-\sqrt{13}$ at $x=123\cdot7^\circ$

(c) 0

7. *(a)* 4

(b) (i) $A_{n+1}=0\cdot75\,A_n+1$; (ii) Yes; since limit is 4 g < 5 g

8. *(a)* Proof $\left\{\text{Hint: use } h=\frac{400}{\pi r^2}\right\}$ *(b)* $r=3\cdot5$ cm approx.

9. *(a)* Proof $\left\{\text{Hint: take } \log_e \text{ of both sides}\right\}$ *(b)* $a=2$; $b=3$

MODEL PAPER G — HIGHER MATHEMATICS ANSWERS

PAPER I

1. *(a)* Proof {show $f(2)=0$ *(b)* $x=-3;\ x=\frac{1}{2}$

2. *(a)* $4y=3x+5$ *(b)* $4x+3y=10$

3. *(a)* 33 units^2 *(b)* Area $= \int_2^5 (2x+4)dx$ *(c)* 33

4. *(a)* $2x+y=-3$ *(b)* B(0, −3) *(c)* C(−2, 1) *(d)* $(x+1)^2+(y+1)^2=5$

5. $\begin{pmatrix} -5 \\ -5 \\ 7 \end{pmatrix}$

6. 

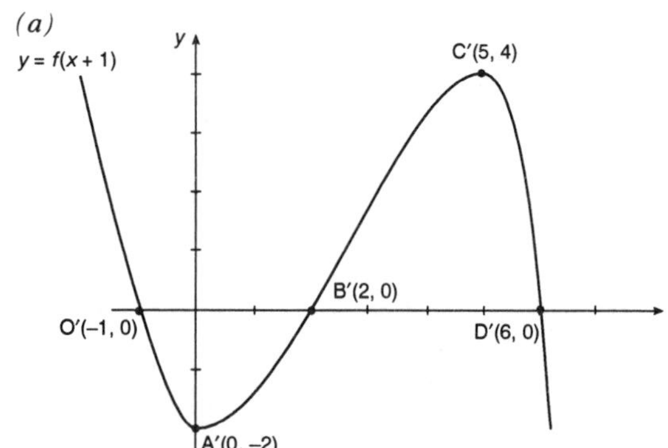

(b)

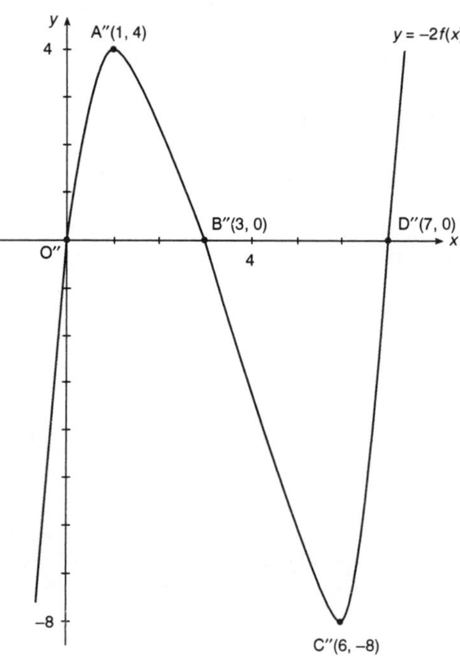

7. $a=-2;\ b=5$

8. *(a)* (i) 9, (ii) 8, (iii) 6 *(b)* 180; $|\boldsymbol{p}| = 6\sqrt{5}$

9. $p=2q$

10. Proof; {show $f'(x)=0$ has no roots}

11. $f'(x)=-2\sin 2x$

PAPER II

1. *(a)* $3x + y = 14$ *(b)* $x + 2y = -2$ *(c)* $(6, -4)$

2. *(a)* $10x + y + 3 = 0$

3. *(a)* $\overrightarrow{AK} = \begin{pmatrix} -5 \\ 5 \\ 11 \end{pmatrix}$ *(b)* $\overrightarrow{AL} = \begin{pmatrix} 2 \\ 4 \\ 9 \end{pmatrix}$ *(c)* $\angle KAL = 34°$ (approx.)

4. *(a)* P(4, 0) *(b)* $x + 2y = 4$ *(c)* $Q\left(\frac{1}{2}, 1\frac{3}{4}\right)$

5. *(a)* (i) $L = 8x + 9y$ (ii) Proof : $\left\{\text{substitute } y = 40 - \frac{8x}{9}\right\}$ *(b)* $x = 22{\cdot}5$; $y = 20$; max area = 2700 m^2

6. *(a)* $k = 0{\cdot}0719$ *(b)* 51·3% reduction

7. *(a)* Proof: {treat OP as the hypotenuse} *(b)* $Q(\cos(a - 45)°, \sin(a - 45)°)$

   (c) $R(\cos(a + 45)°, \sin(a + 45)°)$ *(d)* $m_{QR} = \frac{-1}{\tan a°}$

8. $x = 100{\cdot}2°, 192{\cdot}4°$

9. *(a)* $p = 1$; $q = 2$ *(b)* Area = $2\frac{1}{2}$ units^2

NOTES

QUESTION FREQUENCY CHART FOR HIGHER PAPERS

TOPIC	Paper A		Paper B		Paper C		Paper D		Paper E		Paper F		Paper G	
	I	II	I	II	I	II	I	II	I	II	I	II	I	II
Unit 1														
LO1 The Straight	2			2	3	1		7a	1	1	1	3b	2	1
LO2 $f(x)$, Graphs, Solutions	7	3	2,7		5	4a	4,10	2	2a	5,6a,c	5		6	
LO3 Basic differentation		1	9	7	4.7.11	2a,6	5,9	1	2,4,6	10	4a,9	2,3a,8	10	2,5
LO4 Recurrence relations		5	6			3	6	5		4	7	7	9	
Unit 2														
LO1 Factors, Remainder Theorem, Quadratic	6	4		1,8	1,10	2b	3,7		4,12	1	2,4b	4a	1	4
LO2 Basic, Integration	3	2	1	9		8		8a,b	11	6b	8	4b	3	9
LO3 Trig. form & equations	5,9		8		6		8	6	5	8	6,12			7
LO4 Equation of circle	4		5	4		7	1,12	7b,c	8	2	3	5	4,5	
Unit 3														
LO1 Vectors	1		2,4	3		5	2	3	9	3	11	1	8	3
LO2 Further Calculus	8,9,10	8	11		2	9		4	7,14	9	10		11	
LO3 Logs & exp. function	11	7	10	6	8,9		11		3	7		9	7	6
LO4 Further Trig. & Wave function		6		5	12	4b		8c		5		6		8

Printed by Bell & Bain, Ltd., Glasgow, Scotland, U.K.